CREATIVE
CELEBRATION
cakes

Steve Benison, Lindy Smith
& Linda Wilson-Barker

Edited by CHRISTINE FRANCE
Photography by DON LAST

David & Charles

contents

introduction

Recent years have brought many trends in cake design, and fashions are constantly changing. But today, cake decoration could not be more popular and there is a more diverse range of styles, incorporating a wider range of techniques, than ever before. This book brings together three fine cake artists who are all established in their field, all with very different styles.

These three designers, whose style is distinctively influenced by their varied backgrounds and skills, tastes and travels, show in this book that with creative skill, enthusiasm and imagination, it's possible to create a stunning cake for any occasion. Each of them approaches the cake projects in quite different ways, and you'll find them using techniques and equipment in varied ways to create some very individual effects.

The early chapters of this book begin with useful information on equipment, basic recipes and techniques to get you started, leading on to the cake projects themselves, from formal creations for special occasions to humorous novelty cakes, all illustrated with clear step-by step pictures to guide you. The cakes have been designed to cover all levels of skill, so even if you're a complete beginner there are cakes to give you confidence, yet more experienced confectioners will still find a challenge in some of the more elaborate cakes.

BASIC CAKE *recipes*

RICH FRUIT CAKE

METHOD

1 Preheat the oven to 150°C/300°F/Gas Mark 2. Grease and line the cake tin with a double thickness of greaseproof or non-stick paper. Tie a double thickness of newspaper around the outside to prevent the outside cooking too quickly or unevenly.

2 Mix together the dried fruit, cherries, almonds and lemon zest. Sift the flour with the mixed spice.

3 Cream the butter with the sugar until light and fluffy, then gradually beat in the eggs. Fold in the flour alternately with the fruit and nuts and mix evenly. Stir in the brandy or rum.

4 Spoon the mixture into the tin and level the surface. Place the tin on a double thickness of newspaper in the oven and bake for the time on the chart, reducing the oven temperature to 140°C/275°F/Gas Mark 1 half way through the cooking time. Cooking times may vary with different ovens.

5 When the cake is cooked, it should be just beginning to shrink away from the sides of the tin. To test, insert a skewer into the centre of the cake – if the cake is cooked, it should come out clean, not sticky.

6 Cool the cake completely in the tin,

then turn out and wrap in cling film or a double thickness of greaseproof paper, then foil. Store in a cool, dry place for at least 1 month before use. For extra richness, pierce the cake with a skewer and drizzle over a little extra brandy or rum before storage.

Basic Fruit Cake Recipe

Round	15cm (6in)	18cm (7in)	20cm (8in)	23cm (9in)	25cm (10in)	28cm (11in)	30cm (12in)
Square	13cm (5in)	15cm (6in)	18cm (7in)	20cm (8in)	23cm (9in)	25cm (10in)	28cm (11in)
Mixed dried fruit	400g (14oz)	600g (1lb5oz)	850g (1lb14oz)	1kg (2lb4oz)	1.5kg (3lb5oz)	1.7kg (3lb12oz)	2kg (4lb8oz)
Glacé cherries	50g (1¾oz)	60g (2¼oz)	85g (3oz)	100g (3½oz)	140g (5oz)	175g (6oz)	225g (8oz)
Chopped almonds	40g (1½oz)	50g (2oz)	60g (2½oz)	70g (2½oz)	90g (3¼oz)	115g (4oz)	150g (5½oz)
Lemon zest	2.5ml (½tsp)	5ml (1tsp)	7.5ml (1½tsp)	10ml (2tsp)	15ml (3tsp)	20ml (4tsp)	25ml (5tsp)
Plain flour	140g (5oz)	175g (6oz)	250g (9oz)	375g (13oz)	500g (1lb2oz)	625g (1lb6oz)	750g (1lb10oz)
Mixed spice	2.5ml (½tsp)	5ml (1tsp)	7.5ml (1½tsp)	10ml (2tsp)	15ml (3tsp)	20ml (4tsp)	25ml (5tsp)
Unsalted butter, softened	100g (3½oz)	140g (5oz)	200g (7oz)	280g (10oz)	400g (14oz)	475g (1lb1oz)	550g (1lb4oz)
Dark muscovado sugar	100g (3½oz)	140g (5oz)	200g (7oz)	280g (10oz)	400g (14oz)	475g (1lb1oz)	550g (1lb4oz)
Eggs	2	3	3	4	6	8	8
Brandy or rum	15ml (1tbsp)	25ml (1½tbsp)	30ml (2tbsp)	40ml (2½tbsp)	55ml (3½tbsp)	60ml (4tbsp)	75ml (5tbsp)
Cooking time (approx.)	1¾-2hours	2-2¼hours	2½-3hours	3-3½hours	3½-4hours	4-4½hours	4½-5hours

Note: For oval or hexagonal tins, use the equivalent diameter round cake quantity.
For cake tins of an unusual shape, measure the capacity and use the recipe for an equivalent capacity round tin.

MADEIRA CAKE

TIP

For a moist-textured cake, add 2.5ml (½tsp) glycerine per egg to the mix. Freezing also tends to help make the cake more moist.

METHOD

1 Preheat the oven to 160°C/325°F/Gas Mark 3. Grease and line the cake tin. Sift the flours together.

2 Cream together the butter and sugar until light and fluffy. Beat in the eggs gradually. Fold in the flour, adding a little milk if necessary to make a smooth, dropping consistency.

3 Spoon into the tin and smooth the surface. Bake for the time stated on the chart, until the cake is well risen, golden brown and springy to the touch. Test the cake by inserting a skewer into the centre – it should come out clean.

4 Cool the cake in the tin for 5-10 minutes, then turn out and finish cooling on a wire rack. Store in an airtight tin for up to 2 weeks, or in the freezer for 2 months.

FLAVOURINGS

Vanilla – add a few drops of vanilla essence with the eggs. Citrus – add the finely grated rind of 1 orange or lemon with the eggs. Chocolate – replace one quarter of the plain flour with sifted cocoa.

Basic Madeira Cake Recipe

Round tin	23cm (9in)	25cm (10in)	28cm (11in)	30cm (12in)
Square tin	20cm (8in)	23cm (9in)	25cm (10in)	28cm (11in)
Ball tin	16cm (6¼in)			
Rectangular tin				30.5x20cm (12x8in)
(multi-sized)				30.5x23cm (12x9in)
Self- raising flour	350g (12oz)	450g (1lb)	500g (1lb 2oz)	550g (1lb 4oz)
Plain flour	175g (6oz)	225g (8oz)	250g (9oz)	280g (10oz)
Unsalted butter, softened	350g (12oz)	450g (1lb)	500g (1lb 2oz)	550g (1lb 4oz)
Caster sugar	350g (12oz)	450g (1lb)	500g (1lb 2oz)	550g (1lb 4oz)
Eggs	6	8	9	10
Cooking time (approx)	1¼hr	1¼-1½hr	1½-1¾hr	1¾hr

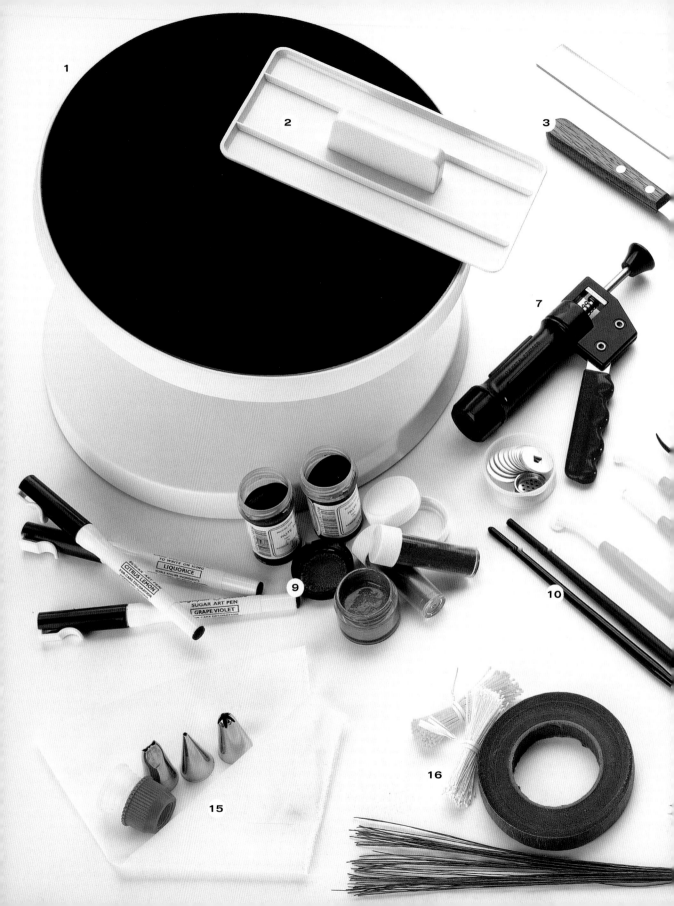

Equipment
and tools

1 **Turntable** choose one which can be tilted, to make side detailing work easier

2 **Smoothing tools** to achieve a smooth surface over sugarpaste or almond paste

3 **Palette knife** a small, angled palette knife is the most useful

4 **Metal ruler and side scraper** for smoothing royal icing to a perfect finish

5 **Foam pad** a soft surface for fine modelling

6 **Rolling pins** for smooth rolling, or textured effects on sugarpaste

7 **Sugar shaper gun** pump with different discs to extrude modelling paste, flower paste or almond paste

8 **Posy picks** for inserting wired flowers into cakes

9 **Colourings** paste, dusting powder and colour pens

10 **Brushes** selection of textures for painting and dusting colour onto icing

11 **Designer or cutting wheel** for cutting or creating effects such as stitching in sugarpaste

12 **Modelling tools** Dresden tool, dog bone tool and ball tool for fine shaping of sugarpaste modelling paste and flower paste

13 **Scalpel** sharp blade for fine cutting, and ribbon insertion blade

14 **Flower cutters** plastic or metal, and plunger cutters for cutting different flower or petal shapes

15 **Piping tubes** a selection of plastic or metal tubes

16 **Florists wire, stamens, tape** varying thicknesses of wire and stamens for different flowers

17 **Tweezers** for fine placing of decoration, especially for flower making

ICING & MODELLING PASTE *recipes*

All of these types of icings and pastes are used throughout this book, and many of them are also sold ready-made or in easy mixes if you prefer not to make your own.

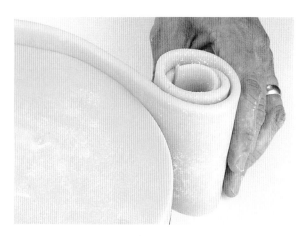

ALMOND PASTE

This is generally used as a base for royal or sugarpaste icing, to give a smooth surface and prevent colour or oil from the cake from staining the icing.

To make 450g (1lb):

225g (8oz) ground almonds

115g (4oz) caster sugar

115g (4oz) icing sugar

1 medium egg

5ml (1tsp) sweet sherry

5ml (1tsp) lemon juice

1.25ml (¼tsp) almond essence

Place the almonds, caster and icing sugars in a large bowl and stir to mix evenly. Beat the egg with the sherry, lemon juice and essence, then stir into the dry ingredients. Turn out onto a work surface and knead gently until smooth, adding a little icing sugar if it becomes too sticky.

Use immediately, or wrap tightly and store in the refrigerator for up to 3 days.

APRICOT GLAZE

Place 115g (4oz) apricot jam in a pan with 30ml (2tbsp) water. Heat gently, stirring until the jam is melted. Bring to the boil, then remove from the heat and press through a fine sieve. Use whilst warm.

BUTTERCREAM

A soft, spreadable icing, usually used for sponge cakes.

To make 350g (12oz):

115g (4oz) unsalted butter, softened

225g (8oz) icing sugar, sifted

2.5ml (½tsp) vanilla essence

15ml (1tbsp) hot water, approx.

Beat the butter with a wooden spoon until smooth and fluffy. Gradually beat in the icing sugar, mixing thoroughly until smooth. Beat in the vanilla essence and enough water to mix to a spreading consistency.

EDIBLE GLUE

Mix 5ml (1tsp) gum Arabic with 15ml (1tbsp) tepid water. Leave for 1 hour. Strain into a screw-topped jar and store in the fridge for up to a week.

SUGAR GLUE

Place a walnut-sized ball of sugarpaste in a saucepan with 30ml (2tbsp) boiled water. Stir over a low heat until dissolved, then bring to the boil. Cool before use.

FLOWER PASTE

5ml (1tsp) white vegetable fat

5ml (1tsp) liquid glucose

225g (8oz) royal icing

15g (½oz) Tylose powder (carboxymethyl cellulose)

Place the fat and glucose in a small bowl over a pan of hot water and stir until just melted. Stir into the royal icing with the Tylose powder, then knead to a firm, stretchy paste.

FLOWER AND MODELLING PASTE

200g (7oz) flower and modelling powder

20ml (4tsp) cold water

10ml (2tsp) white vegetable fat

Place the powder in a bowl and make a well in the centre. Stir in the water and fat then knead until smooth and pliable. Use immediately, or store in an

airtight polythene bag, not cling film, in the refrigerator. Alternatively, freeze for up to 1 month.

FRILLING OR MODELLING PASTE

Knead together 200g (7oz) flower paste with 200g (7oz) white sugarpaste.

PASTILLAGE

This smooth, hard-setting modelling paste can also be obtained as an instant dry-mix that simply requires mixing with water.

10ml (2tsp) white vegetable fat

5ml (1tsp) liquid glucose

500g (1lb 2oz) royal icing

15ml (1tbsp) gum tragacanth

150g (5½oz) icing sugar

Place the fat and glucose in a small bowl over a pan of hot water and stir until just melted. Stir into the royal icing with the gum tragacanth, mixing to a smooth, firm paste. Gradually knead in the icing sugar until it is smooth and elastic. Wrap small portions closely in polythene and store in an airtight container in the refrigerator for 24 hours before use.

ROYAL ICING

This dries to a hard, white finish, ideal for formal designs on rich fruit cakes. It can be used for piping and is particularly suitable for intricate designs such as lacework, flowers or lettering.

To make 900g (2lb):

4 egg whites, or 25g (1oz) albumen powder
   dissolved in 175ml (6fl oz) cold water

900g (2lb) icing sugar, sifted

15ml (1tbsp) lemon juice

***10ml (2tsp) glycerine**

Place the egg whites or albumen in a large bowl. Gradually stir in about half the icing sugar to make a smooth mixture the consistency of cream. Add the remaining sugar gradually, stirring after each

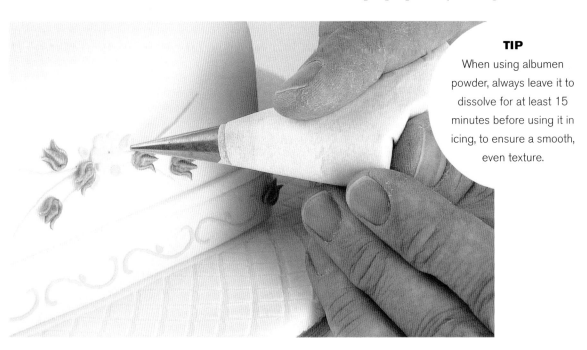

TIP

When using albumen powder, always leave it to dissolve for at least 15 minutes before using it in icing, to ensure a smooth, even texture.

addition, until the mixture holds firm peaks when the spoon is lifted. Beat in the lemon juice.

*Add 10ml (2tsp) glycerine for flat icing, to prevent the icing from becoming too hard, but do not add this if the icing is to be used for piping.

Adjust the thickness by adding more icing sugar for the desired consistency:
- For flat icing, the mixture should hold soft peaks which fall slowly.
- For rough icing or decorative piping, the icing should hold stiff peaks firmly.
- For piping lines or writing, the icing should be between these two consistencies.

Royal icing for piping can be used as soon as it is mixed, but if it is to be used for coating it should be left to stand for about 6 hours or overnight to allow air bubbles to come to the surface. Store in an airtight container.

SUGARPASTE

There are many commercially made ready to use sugarpastes, which come both white and coloured, some with added flavours.

60ml (4tbsp) cold water
20ml (4tsp) powdered gelatine
125ml (4fl oz) liquid glucose
10ml (2tsp) glycerine
1kg (2lb 4oz) icing sugar, sifted

TIP
Many colours will deepen as the paste dries, so if in doubt, try a test piece, then if it darkens on standing you can make the paste a shade lighter than the finished colour you wish to achieve

Place the water in a small bowl and sprinkle over the gelatine, then leave to stand for 5 minutes. Stand the bowl over a pan of hot, not boiling, water and stir until the gelatine is dissolved. Add the glucose and glycerine, stirring until melted. Make a well in the centre of the icing sugar and stir in the liquid ingredients until the mixture binds together. Turn out onto a work surface and knead until smooth and pliable, sprinkling with icing sugar if it becomes too sticky.

Can be used immediately, or tightly wrapped and stored in an airtight container in a cool place for up to 3 days. Knead again before use.

TIP
Sugarpaste is affected by the heat of your hands, so you may need to adjust this by making the paste firmer if your hands are warm.

BASIC *techniques*

These basic techniques will help you to begin making all of the cakes in this book. A wide range of more advanced decorating techniques such as flower-making, modelling and piping are illustrated in the step by steps with each project.

COVERING A CAKE WITH ALMOND PASTE

An easy way to calculate how much almond paste to allow is to weigh the cake - you will need about half the weight of the cake in almond paste to cover the top and sides.

1 Trim the top of the cake if necessary and fill any holes in the cake with small pieces of almond paste. Brush the top with warmed apricot glaze. To cover the cake for a royal icing finish, cut off a third of the almond paste for the top and roll out on a surface lightly dusted with icing sugar to a round large enough for the top of the cake and about 8mm (⅜in) thick. Lift the round onto the cake top and smooth over, trimming and pressing level with the sides of the cake.

TIP

It's a good idea to leave the lining paper on the base of a rich fruit cake where it touches the cake board, to prevent any reaction with the foil covering on the board.

2 Brush the sides of the cake with apricot glaze. Measure the circumference of the cake with string. Roll out the remaining almond paste to the length of the string, about 8mm (⅜in) thick. Roll up lengthways, then carefully unroll onto the sides of the cake. Trim to fit, and smooth over.

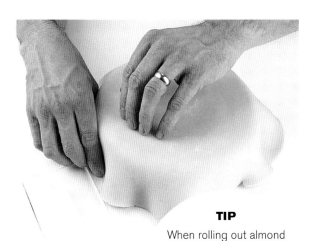

ruler at a 45° angle to the cake and draw it straight across the icing towards you to smooth the surface in one action. Trim surplus from edges and allow to dry.

TIP
When rolling out almond paste, use icing sugar rather than cornflour, as the latter may ferment with the natural yeasts in the sugar on the almond paste.

3 To cover a cake with almond paste for a sugarpaste finish, roll out the total amount of almond paste and lift carefully over the cake with a rolling pin. Unroll onto the cake, then ease around the sides and smooth to fit, trimming off the excess.

2 Place the cake on a turntable. Spread the remaining two thirds of icing around the sides with the palette knife as before. Hold a straight-sided icing comb against the side at a 45° angle and draw the comb over the side to smooth the icing, turning the turntable with the other hand. For a square cake, apply each side separately. Leave to dry.

COVERING A CAKE WITH ROYAL ICING
Building up a smooth, even coating of royal icing takes time and patience, as each layer must be dried out for at least 24 hours before adding the next. Two layers is the minimum, and the more layers you add, the easier it will be to achieve a perfectly smooth surface.

1 Put about a third of the icing for the first layer on top of the cake and spread with a palette knife, using a paddling action to eliminate air bubbles. Hold an icing

3 To cover the board with icing, spread an even layer of icing over the top surface of the board with a palette knife. Use a straight-sided comb to smooth off the icing, turning the turntable as you go.

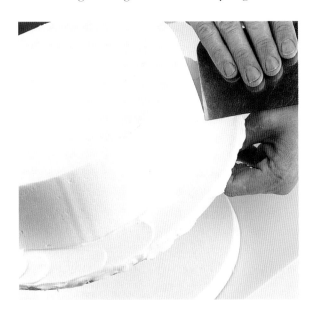

TIP

If you don't have an icing turntable, improvise by placing a mixing bowl upside down on the work surface, topped with an upturned plate to put the cake onto. The inner rim of the plate must fit the base of the bowl neatly so that it can turn easily and safely.

COVERING A CAKE WITH SUGARPASTE

Sugarpaste gives a smooth, firm surface with just one coat.

1 Brush the almond paste with clear alcohol, then roll out the sugarpaste and lift over the cake on rolling pin, smoothing to avoid creases. Trim surplus paste, keeping the palette knife vertical to the cake side to avoid undercutting. Smooth the surface with a plastic smoother. Polish with a small piece of sugarpaste for a satin smooth finish. Allow to dry for 24 hours.

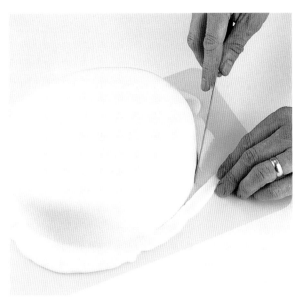

2 To cover the board with sugarpaste, roll out a band of paste to the same width as the uncovered edge of board. Brush the board with alcohol to moisten, then lift the paste onto it and smooth to finish, pressing the joins to seal neatly. Trim the edge with a sharp knife.

TIP

Brushing the almond paste with alcohol helps to give a sticky surface for the sugarpaste to adhere to. If you prefer not to use alcohol, use a sugar syrup made by dissolving sugar in an equal amount of water and cooled.

MAKING A PAPER ICING BAG

1 Cut a 25cm (10inch) square of greaseproof paper or non-stick baking parchment. Cut it in half diagonally to make two triangles.

2 Take the right hand point of one triangle and curl it over to meet the middle point, as shown.

3 Take the opposite point across the first and round the back to meet at the middle point, making a pointed cone shape.

4 Hold the points together and fold over firmly twice to keep in place. To use, snip off the tip and use for plain writing without a nozzle, or snip off the tip and place a nozzle inside before filling with icing.

TIP

Take care not to overfill the icing bag – about half-full is enough, so you're left with plenty of paper to fold over and seal at the top.

GRADUATION
party

This spectacular parcel cake bursting

with a bright new future for a new

graduate is a perfect choice for a

happy family occasion such as a

graduation. The cake itself is very

simple, and with careful modelling

even a beginner should be able to

achieve an impressive result.

Ingredients

18cm (7in) square cake covered with yellow sugarpaste on a 25cm (10in) square cake board covered in purple sugarpaste

150g (5½oz) white frilling paste

100g (3½oz) pastillage

Paste colours:
baby blue, pink, primrose, liquorice black, purple

Edible silver paint

Liquorice black food pen

Cream powder colour

Edible glue

1 Measure lengths of wired silver ribbon to fit from the base of one side of the cake up and over the base on the opposite side, plus 5cm (2in). Feed one end of a ribbon under the centre of the cake base, over the cake top, down and under the opposite side, easing with a palette knife. Repeat with the remaining two sides. Cut a small hole in the ribbon at the cross over point in the cake centre. Insert two posy picks through the ribbon cut.

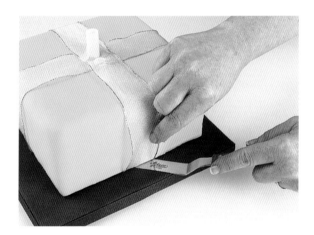

2 Loop lengths of ribbon and secure at the base with white florist wire. Tape with white floral tape to neaten. Make three or four of these and insert into one of the posy picks.

3 To make scrolls, roll a length of white frilling paste into a thin sausage. Snip into 1cm (½in) lengths with scissors. Roll white frilling paste thinly and cut a rectangle 8cm x 5cm (3¼in x 2in). Soften the edges with a dog bone tool on a foam pad. Place one sausage shape onto one side of the rectangle. Roll up the scroll firmly, securing the end with glue. Cut a narrow strip of purple frilling paste and fix around the centre of the scroll to form a tie. Insert a glued, hooked 22g wire into the centre of the scroll and dry. Dust the edges with ivory powder colour and inscribe with a food pen.

Tools and Equipment

4m (4¼yds) x 4cm (1½in) wired edge silver ribbon

Palette knife

2 posy picks

22g white florist wire

White floral tape

Dog bone tool

Scalpel

Small designer wheel

4cm (1½in) round cutter

4cm (1½in) square cutter

1.5m (1¾yds) silver cord

4 For the books, cut a 2.5cm (1in) square from white frilling paste 5mm (¼in) thick. Etch three sides with a scalpel for book pages. Cut a 5cm x 3cm (2 x 1¼in) rectangle from thinly rolled coloured frilling paste. Mark stitching around all sides with a designer wheel. Place the white square on one side fixing with glue and fold the opposite side over. Insert a 22g white wire (dipped in glue) into either the base of the book or the side. Leave to dry. Use food pens for the lettering. Paint the page edges with edible silver paint.

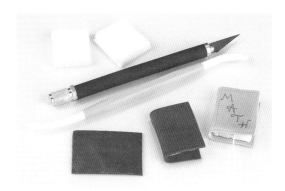

5 For the mortarboards, roll black frilling paste to 3mm (⅛in) thick and cut a 4cm (1½in) circle. Pinch to form four corners, turn over and glue in a large pea size of black paste. Cut a 4cm (1½in) black square, and place on a non-stick surface. Apply glue to the centre and fix the cap in place, offsetting the corners. Insert a hooked glued 22g white wire and dry upside down. For tassels, roll out yellow frilling paste very thinly. Cut 3cm (1¼in) squares and make cuts into the length leaving a small edge. Roll up from one end. Glue on to the mortarboards. Insert the wired decorations into the second posy pick, arranging loops around. Fix silver cord around the cake.

Variation

For a special birthday cake for someone who loves to sew, transform it into a 'buttons and bows' cake. Cut out small flower buttons and bows from coloured frilling paste and fix to wires as in main instructions. Brush with confectioner's varnish when dry. Mould thimbles from frilling paste or pastillage in a bell mould with tulle for texture, paint with edible silver colour and fix to wires as above.

ANNIE *apple*

This jolly apple character would be a wonderful birthday

surprise for any birthday boy or girl, but it's particularly good

for toddlers and younger children and could be adapted for

other favourite fruits in other bright colours. It's a good one for

a newcomer to sugarpaste modelling, too, needing no special

skills, just a good creative eye and careful shaping.

Ingredients

6-egg madeira cake baked in a 16cm (6¼in) ball tin

Buttercream

1.3kg (3lb) sugarpaste

200g (7oz) modelling paste

White powder colour

Paste colours: yellow, olive green, fresh green, burgundy, red and brown

Clear alcohol *eg* gin

Sugar glue

White vegetable fat

1 Have a real apple in front of you to refer to. If the cake has been cooked in two halves, level each cake and stick together with buttercream. Freeze the cake. Using a large knife, remove some of the fullness from the lower half of the ball (see carving guide p.106). Next remove a cone from the top to make a recess for the stalk, then shape the upper edge of the apple. Place on waxed paper and spread thinly with buttercream.

TIP
Mixing white dust into paste colour gives a thicker consistency to the colour, so it behaves like an acrylic paint rather than a watercolour and will fill any crazing or small indentations in the surface of sugarpaste.

2 Colour 500g (1lb 2oz) sugarpaste yellow. Cover the board. Leave to dry. Colour the remaining sugarpaste pale yellow-green using some yellow trimmings and green paste colour. Roll out and place over the cake, easing around the base, and pull up the excess paste to form a pleat. Cut the pleat away, smoothing the join. Trim the excess from the base and smooth the surface. Mix the green paste colours with white dust and alcohol, and apply with a flat-headed brush in vertical strokes. Leave to dry. Mix the red paste colour with white dust to a thick paint. Using a dry large headed brush, apply very lightly to sections of the apple in long vertical strokes. Dry, then place on the board.

3 For the nose, take some of the yellow sugarpaste trimmings and roll into a 2.5cm (1in) ball. Stick in place with sugar glue and flatten slightly to secure. For the mouth, roll out 20g (¾oz) red modelling paste between the narrow spacers. Place the template (p.106) on the paste and cut around it with a cutting wheel. Stick in position, then add the corners to the mouth modelled from thinly rolled paste.

Tools and Equipment

23cm (9in) round cake board

Waxed paper

Rolling pin

Smoother

Large flat headed
paintbrush

Large headed brush
eg shaving brush

Narrow spacers from
1.5mm (⅛in) card

Cutting wheel

Cutters: 3.5cm (1⅜in) oval
and 2cm (¾in) round

Small scissors

Pieces of foam for support

Leaf veiner or real leaf

Ribbon

4 Colour the remaining modelling paste: 130g (4¾oz) bright green, 20g (¾oz) black and 10g (¼oz) brown, leaving the rest white. For the eyes, roll out black and white modelling pastes using spacers. Cut two ovals from the white and two circles from the black pastes. Place the black circles on top of the white ovals, add a light spot of the white paste then roll the pastes together between the spacers. Re-cut the eyes with the oval cutters and glue to the face. Add eyebrows modelled from the green trimmings.

Variation

For a more adult birthday cake, change the facial features to sexy red bow lips and fluttery lashes, shaped from the modelling paste. Or, change the fruit to a tomato or orange instead.

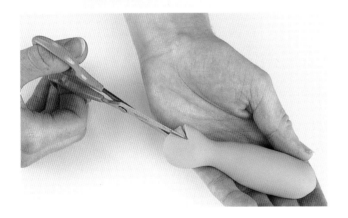

5 Divide green modelling paste into four. For feet, roll two cones, flatten slightly and attach to the base of the apple. Roll two into sausages, thin at one end to form wrists by rolling them between your fingers. With small scissors, cut a triangle from each to form thumbs. Cut the upper arms at an angle to fit neatly onto the body. Glue in place, supporting with foam. Make a stem from brown paste and glue to the cake. Roll out the remaining green paste thinly and cut a leaf shape. Vein with a veiner tool or real leaf. Glue to the stem and support it in place with the foam until dry. Attach the ribbon around the board.

On Your
Retirement
Andrew

RETIREMENT *cake*

A pretty garden theme is often a very appropriate choice for the celebration of a retirement, with a door on the garden arch opening to new and pleasant challenges. This type of cake is easy to tailor to suit an individual, as favourite flowers, vegetables or garden features can be incorporated into the design.

Ingredients

20cm (8in) round rich fruit cake, covered with pale green sugarpaste on

30cm (12in) cake board, covered with sugarpaste

600g (1lb 5oz) sugarpaste

175g (6oz) pastillage

Royal icing

Paste colours: stone, terracotta, green

Powder colours: rustic browns, terracotta, green

Sugar glue

White vegetable fat

1 Take approximately 55g (2oz) each of pastillage and sugarpaste and mix together to a light stone colour. Roll out then allow to rest for a few minutes. Turn the paste over and cut out the paving slabs using the two sizes of square cutters.

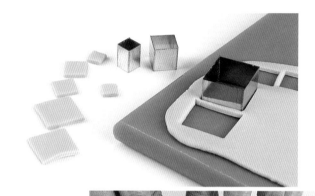

2 Trace or photocopy onto thin cardboard the circle template (p.108), which is used as a divisional guide to show the position of the paving slabs and also for the base of the arch. Place this onto the surface of the cake, securing the paving slabs in position with a dab of royal icing. Repeat on the cake board so that the paving corresponds with those on the top of the cake.

3 Trace the arch and door template (p.108) onto thin cardboard then place this onto thinly rolled out pastillage. Cut out the pieces with a scalpel. Place the door inside the archway to dry on a drying board. Turn the sections over during drying and clean the edges with sandpaper prior to painting.

Tools and Equipment

Small square and
oval cutters

Circle, arch, door and gate
templates

Thin card

Paintbrushes

Scalpel

Sandpaper

Small scissors

Wooden dowel/skewer

Overhead projector film

Spaghetti

Plastic drinking straw

No.1 piping tube

Scriber

1.25m (1½yards)
terracotta ribbon

4 Brush a little powder colour over the surface, then dilute with water to make a combination of lighter and darker tones of rustic browns and terracotta. Paint on the token-effect brick work. Use a piece of cardboard to paint the panels of the door, moving the edge of the card towards yourself as you paint, leaving a small gap between each panel. Turn over and paint the reverse.

5 Shape a cherry-sized piece of pastillage over the end of a wooden dowel to form the flowerpots. Make two cuts opposite each other with scissors, then cut across the base to make the two halves. The larger pot, which will help to support the door arch, has a band of paste around the rim. Make a second pot slightly smaller, for the opposite side of the door arch.

6 Photocopy the gate template (p.108) onto paper. Place under the transparency film, held in place with masking tape. Carefully cut out the stencil with a scalpel. Roll out the pale cream modelling paste. Lightly rub the surface with a little white fat, then place the cut-out stencil over. Use a flat paintbrush to brush powder colour over. Remove the stencil carefully. Cut around the gate and secure with glue on the side of the cake (see p.26 for position). Repeat for the remaining five gates.

7 Colour the remaining sugarpaste pale green. Roll out to a band and apply texture using a lattice design roller. Measure the space between each gate. Cut a strip of paste measuring 4cm (1½in) deep. Place an oval cutter onto the top edge and cut out a small ellipse, securing the concave piece of paste onto the side of the cake with glue.

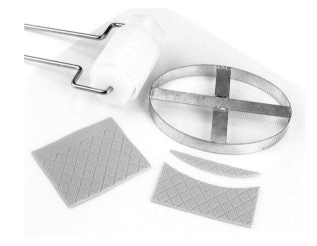

8 Brush the flowerpots with terracotta powder colour. For the two trees, which are standing upright, roll a small sausage of pastillage for the trunk, inserting a piece of spaghetti through the centre for added support. Shape foliage from green paste, using a flattened plastic drinking straw to give texture. Secure the tree trunks onto the side of the cake with glue and add the foliage and the half flowerpots. Pipe small dots of soft royal icing for a flower effect.

9 Paint the trailing ivy leaves onto the brickwork using green powder colour diluted with water.

10 Make a tracing of the inscription (p.108) and secure this onto the sugarpaste covering. Hold it in position with small pieces of masking tape. Scribe each letter then overpipe with soft royal icing.

Variation

For a gardening-lover's birthday cake, replace the piped message with cut out lettering secured to a round pastillage plaque. Indent the edges with a small cutter to decorate. This plaque could take the place of the arch. Add tiny modelled or piped flowers and vegetables to the garden for variation.

11 Pipe soft royal icing at the base of the archway and secure into position on the cut out pastillage circle. Secure each of the flowerpots onto the base, piping a little icing onto the foliage to help to support the arch. Attach the door with a little royal icing, removing surplus with a small damp paintbrush. Attach the ribbon around the board.

SKATEBOARDING
soccer player

What young boy wouldn't go for this

sporty guy, complete with his team's own

strip and a trendy skateboard? It's

colourful, fun, and suitable for most ages

of children – just adapt it for their

favourite sport or team colours. Once

you've mastered the basic cutting of the

cake shapes, the rest is easy – just be

creative!

Ingredients

8 egg (9in) square
maderia cake

Buttercream

Sugarpaste:
1.8kg (4lb) green
475g (1lb 1oz) red
350g (12oz) white

175g (6oz) black
200g (7oz) flesh

Modelling paste:
25g (1oz) red
55g (2oz) black
55g (2oz) white
55g (2oz) grey

White vegetable fat

Sugar glue

Silver liquid colour

1 Cover the board with green sugarpaste. Press a clean pan scourer firmly into the soft sugarpaste to create textured grass. There are many types of scourers, so experiment to see which effect you like best. Once you are happy with the effect, trim the sugarpaste flush with the edges of the board and leave to dry.

2 Trim the cake crust and level to 6cm (2½in) high. Place all the template pieces (p.103) onto the cake and cut vertically around each. Freeze the cakes until firm. For the body, reduce the height of the neck to 3.5cm (1¼in) by slicing up from the neck to the lower edge of the shirt, then curve the side edges. Level the sleeve and trouser cakes to a height of 3.5cm (1¼in) and curve the side edges. Level the head cake to 5cm (2in) high and carve away the top to make an oval face. Level the ball cake to 4.5cm (1¾in) high. Round the top edges to a dome then cut around the base to form the ball.

TIP
Freezing the cakes makes shaping the cake a lot easier, but if you are pushed for time omit this stage.

Tools and Equipment

46 x 40cm (18 x 16in) rectangular cake board

Waxed paper

Pan scourer for texturing

Templates

Narrow spacers made from stiff card

Smoother

Palette knife

Sugar shaper

Paintbrush

Ball tool

3cm (1¼in) (point to point) hexagonal cutter

Ribbon

3 Place the shirt cake on waxed paper and spread the top with buttercream. Cover in red sugarpaste, smooth and trim around the sides and the neck, cutting flush with the shirt base. Lift onto the board. Spread buttercream over the shirt base. Roll more red paste and cut one edge straight. Cover the shirt base, placing the straight edge against the board, smooth and cut flush with the top of the shirt. Place the sleeves on waxed paper and spread the top with buttercream. Cover with red sugarpaste, trim and place at the top of the shirt. Spread buttercream on the base of the arms. Roll out red paste and cut one edge straight. Place the edge against the board on the uncovered part of the sleeve sections. Smooth and trim. Cover the trouser legs and ball with white sugarpaste.

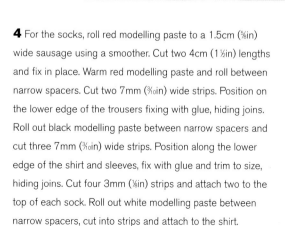

TIP

Rolling out sugarpaste on a surface smeared with white fat rather than icing sugar will ensure that there are no unwanted white marks on the sugarpaste.

4 For the socks, roll red modelling paste to a 1.5cm (⅝in) wide sausage using a smoother. Cut two 4cm (1½in) lengths and fix in place. Warm red modelling paste and roll between narrow spacers. Cut two 7mm (⅜in) wide strips. Position on the lower edge of the trousers fixing with glue, hiding joins. Roll out black modelling paste between narrow spacers and cut three 7mm (⅜in) wide strips. Position along the lower edge of the shirt and sleeves, fix with glue and trim to size, hiding joins. Cut four 3mm (⅛in) strips and attach two to the top of each sock. Roll out white modelling paste between narrow spacers, cut into strips and attach to the shirt.

5 Place the face on waxed paper, spread with buttercream and cover with flesh sugarpaste. Trim and position on the board. Allow to dry. For hair, roll black modelling paste between narrow spacers. Paint glue over the top of the head. Cut black paste into strips and position over the glue. For the eyes, roll two small balls of black paste, elongate into cones and glue to the face. Make a smile from softened red paste in a sugar shaper and glue in place. Using flesh coloured paste, attach a small ball for the nose. For ears, attach two 1.5cm (⅝in) balls and press the lower edge of each to create a wedge. Roll 4.5cm (1¾in) long arms and fix in place. Add elongated balls for hands.

6 For the boots, slightly elongate two 3cm (1¼in) wide balls of black modelling paste, pinch one end to form the top of the boot and the other to form the toes. Stick in place with sugar glue so the boots are parallel with the edges of the board. Gently but firmly press the smoother on to the sole of the boots to flatten and if necessary, adjust their position. Add strips of white trim for decoration.

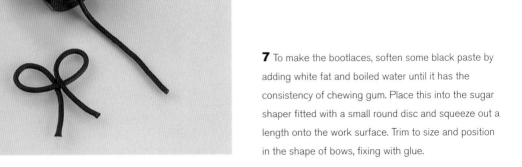

7 To make the bootlaces, soften some black paste by adding white fat and boiled water until it has the consistency of chewing gum. Place this into the sugar shaper fitted with a small round disc and squeeze out a length onto the work surface. Trim to size and position in the shape of bows, fixing with glue.

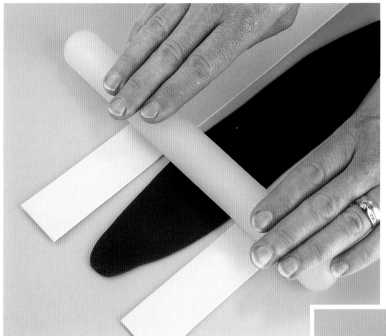

8 For the ball, roll out black and white modelling pastes between narrow spacers. Cut hexagons from the white paste. Place five cut shapes onto the black paste to indicate the edges of the black pentagon. Mark the pentagon, remove the shapes then cut out the pentagon and glue in place on top of the ball. Arrange five hexagons around the central pentagon. Cut the black pentagon shapes slightly larger than required. Place below the joins in the hexagons. Position the next hexagon below one of the first five and adjust the cut of the black paste. Continue until the ball is covered. Lift onto the board.

9 Roll grey modelling paste to 5mm (¼in) thick. Cut to a 20 x 3cm (8 x 1¼in) strip and curve the corners. Paint glue on one long edge and position the strip on the sole of the foot, parallel to the edge of the board, fixing vertically. Turn up the ends of the skateboard. Make dark grey modelling paste from grey and black paste. Roll two 1.5cm (⅝in) wide, 2.5cm (1in) long sausages and roll the centre of each between your fingers to resemble dumbbells. Glue in place. Indent the centre of each wheel with the small end of a ball tool and place a small black ball of paste in each. Paint the uppermost edge of the skateboard with silver. Attach the ribbon.

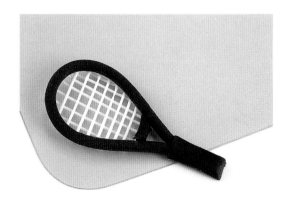

Variation

If the birthday boy – or girl - is fond of another sport, vary the items and instead shape a tennis racquet, rugby ball, cricket or baseball bat, surfboard, American football or scooter. Or, personalise the cake by changing the team colours to those of his favourite team. For a simpler version, make a square cake and cover in green textured sugarpaste, then cut the shapes for the soccer player and assemble flat as a two-dimensional picture to the cake.

DASHING
THROUGH
the **snow**

Children of all ages will love these cute

animal characters tobogganing over the

freshly fallen snow in their teacup sleigh,

and they can even help to model the

characters. Youngsters rarely go for rich

fruit cakes or almond paste, so the

chocolate alternative with buttercream

and sugarpaste makes a welcome change

to a traditional fruit Christmas cake.

Ingredients

25cm (10in) oval chocolate madeira cake

500g (1lb 2oz) buttercream

140g (5oz) raspberry jam

1.3 kg (3lb) sugarpaste

Royal icing

175g (6oz) pastillage

225g (8oz) modelling paste

Paste food colours: chestnut brown, sunflower, hydrangea blue, leaf green, holly ivy, Christmas red

White powder colour

Edible silver colour

Confectioner's varnish

Sugar glue

Clear alcohol *eg* gin

White vegetable fat

1 Cut the cake with a serrated knife making angled cuts diagonally across the cake. Scoop out the two pieces from each side and position on the surface, helping to create the peaks and shallows of the snow effect. Soften the edges of the cake by trimming, giving a rounded appearance.

2 Smooth the buttercream over the surface of the cake, taking care not to disturb too much of the loose cake crumbs. Fill any indentations to provide an even surface for the sugarpaste.

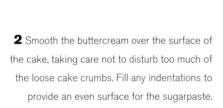

3 Knead the sugarpaste lightly and roll out on a surface lightly dusted with icing sugar. Use spacers to ensure an even thickness. Lift the paste carefully onto the rolling pin then drape over the cake. Smooth with your hands, trim the surplus paste from the base of the cake, then polish with a small ball of paste to give a satin smooth finish. Make an indentation with the cup into the fresh sugarpaste covering.

Tools and Equipment

Serrated knife	Masking tape	Snowflake template
Palette knife	Cocktail sticks	Run-out film
35cm (14in) oval cake board	Scissors	No. 1 piping tube
China cup	Ball tool	Soft brush
2 tea spoons	Dresden tool	Side design roller
Fine sandpaper	No.1 paintbrush	1.25m (1½yards) red ribbon

4 Colour ¾ of the pastillage pale blue. Lightly dust inside of cup with cornflour. Make a hollow in the paste with your thumb. Using your thumb, gradually work from the base to the rim of the cup as you thin the paste, trimming off the excess. It is advisable to remove the paste and re-dust with a little cornflour as you work to prevent sticking. Leave the pastillage inside the cup for at least 12 hours to harden, then remove to finish drying.

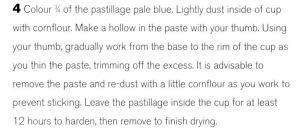

5 Make the spoons by rolling out a sausage of paste, flatten the end, then place on a metal tea spoon to continue shaping. Thin the edges of the spoon and trim with scissors to neaten. Make the handle from a sausage of paste and flattened with your fingers. Depending on the style of the cup, it may be easier to shape the handle against the china cup to get the exact curve, before placing on a drying surface.

6 Remove the dry pastillage cup, and carefully clean the edges with fine sandpaper. Apply a band of masking tape around the side of the cup then paint fine lines on either side of the masking tape. Remove the tape. Paint the spoons with edible silver food colouring. If you use a powder, mix it with clear alcohol then paint over the spoons. When dry, paint over with a thin coat of confectioners varnish to seal.

7 Colour the modelling paste a light brown for the heads of the characters. Start by taking a round of paste the size of walnut. Form a sausage of paste and insert a cocktail stick down through the centre. Make a hollow in the ball of paste then insert the sausage of paste forming the neck and part torso. Using a ball tool make the indents for eyes, and use your fingers to shape a nose. Shape the eye using a Dresden tool. Hollow the mouth, inserting a small piece of pale pink paste and finally two white teeth.

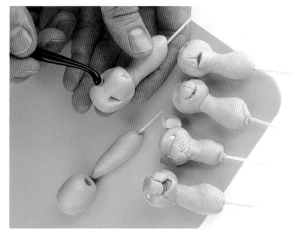

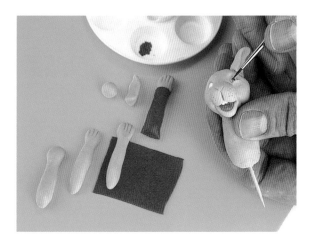

8 Shape ears from small pea sizes of paste, hollowing out the centre, then secure to the head with glue. For the rabbit, make the ears longer and gently pinch the edges to thin. Paint on the white fur effect after all the shaping is complete. For the arms, make a sausage of modelling paste, flatten one end and mark with a palette knife to make four fingers. Roll out the coloured paste for the sleeve, place on the shaped arm, bringing the edges of the paste together and cut with scissors, sealing the two cut edges.

TIP
Rub a little white vegetable fat on your hands before kneading colourings into sugarpaste, to prevent the colour from staining your fingers.

9 Roll out the coloured modelling paste and cut into a rectangle long enough to go around the torso of the character. Fold the top edge over creating a roll top sweater. Cover the torso making the join at the back and trim as you did with the sleeve.

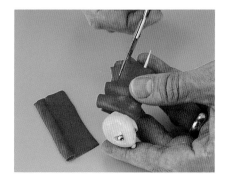

10 To make hats, shape coloured paste into a ball and hollow the centre with a ball tool. Mark the indentations using the edge of a small palette knife. Form the peak of the hat from a flattened sausage of paste, attaching with glue. Make the other hat from a small rectangle of paste with one edge folded over, and the opposite edge gathered to make a cone shape. Secure a small ball of paste on top. For the scarf, cut a strip of paste then cut the tassels at one end before drying on a crumpled piece of cling film.

11 Roll out a band of paste to go round the side of the cake. Using the side design roller apply a ribbed texture, then attach to the cake. Pipe the design above the band using a no.1 tube with soft red royal icing.

12 Place the snowflake template (p.110) under a piece of clear run-out film and lightly rub the surface with a little white vegetable fat to ease removal. Using a no.1 piping tube with white royal icing, pipe over the template and allow to dry for at least 12 hours. When dry, lightly brush surface with sugar glue then sprinkle with white sparkle colour. Brush powder blue colouring over the surface of the cake with a large soft brush to give shadows to the snow.

TIP

To make your own sparkle white, brush egg white onto run-out film, allow to dry then flake into a small container. Either add lustre powder, or leave it a natural colour.

Variation

To simplify the cake if time is short at the festive season, shape just two simple characters (the children may like to help with this), then tuck them straight into a pile of sugarpaste 'snow' instead of the teacup.

13 Colour sugarpaste pale blue to three-quarters fill the dry pastillage cup. Shape inside of the cup on a 45° angle. Make four hollows in the sugarpaste for the characters. Carefully remove the cocktail sticks from each character, twisting as you pull out. Adjust the positions to ensure the faces can be seen. Secure the cup to the cake with royal icing. Attach the handle with a sugar gunge (pastillage mixed with a little sugar glue: much stronger and a better colour match). Attach the spoons and snowflakes and fix a band of ribbon around the board.

BERTHA
THE BATHING
beauty

A summer birthday cake with a sense

of humour, Bertha makes sure there

are ample portions for all! Shaping the

cakes takes a little practice, and you

should allow plenty of time for

creating the colourful decoration.

The realistic hair is achieved by

using a sugar shaper.

Ingredients

10 egg 28cm (11in)
square madeira cake

Buttercream

2 kg (4lb 8oz) sugarpaste:
1.2kg (2lb 10oz) flesh colour
800g (1lb 2oz) white

Modelling paste:
400g (14oz) deep pink
75g (3oz) orange
75g (3oz) yellow
15g (1/2oz) black

Sugar glue

White vegetable fat

Paste colours:
pink, orange, yellow,
blue and brown

Dust colour: peach

Piping gel

1 Trim the crust from the cake base, level the top and cut in half vertically. Spread the top of one half with buttercream and stack on the other half. Freeze until firm. Position the top template (p.104) and cut around it vertically. Place the profile template (p.105) on one long side of the cake and cut around for the basic body shape, marking the position of the arms and head. Curve and shape the cut edges. Cut the head from the body. Place the body in position on the board, spread with buttercream and cover with flesh sugarpaste. Smooth and trim. Mark fingers on the hands with a Dresden tool. Use the other end of the tool to mark fingernails. Place the head on waxed paper, spread with buttercream, cover with sugarpaste, smooth and trim. Fix in position and dry.

TIP
To make a realistic flesh colour use brown with a touch of orange and pink.

2 Knead the pink paste and roll it between narrow spacers. Paint glue over the body where costume will go. Cover the body, smooth and trim. Shape the costume top by removing paste from the back to form straps and cut away around the arms. Cut random circles (we've shown this flat for clarity, but your costume will already be on the cake). Roll out orange paste slightly thicker than the pink. Cut rounds with three cutters, place into the holes on the costume and smooth to fit. Paint glue around the straps. Soften orange paste and squeeze from the sugar shaper with a medium round disc. Trim to fit and smooth into place around the neck and armholes.

3 For eyelashes, paint two curved lines of glue on the face. Roll out black modelling paste and cut into a strip. Thin one edge of the strip then cut out small triangles of paste to create lashes. Cut excess paste from behind the lashes and stick in place, adjusting the curve. Dust the cheeks with peach dust colour. For the bandanna, roll out orange modelling paste between narrow spacers and cut a 2.5cm x 30cm (1in x 12in) strip. Attach around the head, gathering two ends on one side. Fix a thin strip of pink modelling paste to the lower edge. Shape ears and nose from flesh sugarpaste and fix in place.

Tools and Equipment

33cm x 28cm (13in x 11in) oval cake board

Waxed paper

Dresden tool

Narrow spacers made from stiff card

Craft knife

Cutting wheel

Round cutters: 5mm, 1cm and 1.5cm (¼in, ⅜in and ⅝in)

Sugar shaper

Paintbrushes

Ribbon

TIP

To soften modelling paste for the sugar shaper, add a little white fat and boiled water, then knead until it is the consistency of chewing gum.

4 For the hair, soften yellow modelling paste and place in the sugar shaper fitted with a large mesh disc. Paint glue over the top of the head and below the bandanna at the back. Squeeze out approximately 1.5cm (⅝in) lengths of paste, remove with a Dresden tool and attach, covering the head completely. For the bandanna tie, cut oval shaped pieces from orange modelling paste and edge each with a thin pink strip. Stick ties over the gathered join in the bandanna and finish off a small orange ball for the knot.

5 For the sea, colour the remaining white sugarpaste a range of blues. Roughly knead together then cut the paste in half to reveal the marbled pattern inside. Place the 2 halves next to each other, cut side uppermost, and rub the join closed. Roll out the paste and cut into two strips and wrap these strips around Bertha, adjusting as necessary. Smooth the joins closed and trim to fit the board. Leave to dry.

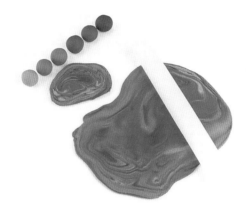

Variation

For a really special friend or family member's birthday, you could personalise the hair and facial features, or add a favourite sunhat made from modelling paste. Or, make a male version of Bertha for a very special fella! Add extra detail to the water such as fish heads or tails made from modelling paste.

6 With a large paintbrush apply piping gel to the board so that the water becomes reflective and the colours intensify. Pour some gel on to the board and paddle it with your brush to remove any lumps before spreading. Once the board is covered run the brush through the gel to create ripples. Finally, attach a ribbon around the board.

RUBY
WEDDING
anniversary

Forty years of happy marriage is something well worth a formal

celebration, and this eye-catching cake will be a real talking

point. Covered with softly marbled sugarpaste and topped with

ruby-red roses, the main skills called for are for modelling

the roses, but with a little practice they can be made to

look almost like the real thing!

Ingredients

20cm (8in) round cake, covered with ivory sugarpaste on

30cm (12in) octagonal board, covered with sugarpaste

200g (7oz) ivory frilling paste

200g (7oz) flower and modelling paste

200g (7oz) pastillage

Powder colours: ivory pearl lustre, burgundy, moss, red

Paste colours: eucalyptus, liquorice black, ivory, Christmas red, spruce green

Rejuvenator spirit

Edible glue

Royal icing

1 Mix a small amount of ivory paste colour with rejuvenator spirit, dip in a piece of sea sponge. Dab all over the board and cake. Next paint fine lines in a crazed pattern with the same colour. Before it is dry, brush over from side to side with a flat, soft bristle brush to produce a marbled effect.

2 For the roses, cut a one third length of 20g moss green wire and cover with half width moss tape. Mould a large grape sized piece of flower paste (colour to match the rose). Roll one side of the ball of paste to a point. Measure the cone against the centre of the petal of the 9cm (3½in) one piece blossom. The cone should be the same length as the blossom petal width. Dry the cone thoroughly.

TIP
When modelling flowers, roll out only enough paste to cut a few petals at a time, and keep it covered, as flower paste dries out quickly.

Tools and Equipment

Small piece of sea sponge	T12 veiner	Dresden tool	Ribbon
Soft brush	7cm (2¾in) square x 1cm (⅜in) thick piece of foam	13cm (5in) white or ivory cake pillar	
20g green wire	Large calyx cutter	Ribbed rolling pin	
Green tape	Dog bone tool	Textured rolling pin	
9cm (3½in) 5-petal blossom cutter	Rose leaf cutter and veiner	Wired crystal-look beads	

3 Roll the flower paste thinly and cut four sets of 9cm (3½in) blossom. Roll the blossom on each petal with a T12 veiner, concentrating particularly on thinning the edges. Place the blossom on the foam. Push the dry cone through the centre of both blossom and foam, holding firmly beneath the foam. Brush all petals with glue. Bring the back petal upwards attaching to the cone, bringing the petal sides around the cone. The top should be quite closed with no visible cone. Repeat with alternate petals. Remove the foam. Apply the second blossom in the same way.

4 Vein the third blossom as the first. Place on foam and use a small rolling pin to roll the top of each petal towards the centre for a curled effect. Turn the blossom over and gently press the centre with the end of a small rolling pin to cup slightly. Push the rose bud on wire through both blossom and foam. Brush the petals half way up from centre with glue, lining up the bud seam with the centre of one petal. Wrap petals one and three around the bud, securing half way up only. Complete with petals five, two and four. Attach the fourth blossom in the same way. Leave to dry.

5 Roll a small amount of dark green flower paste and white paste very thinly. Lay the white paste onto the green and firmly roll together. Cut out a large calyx shape. With scissors make a small cut down the side of each sepal towards the base. Place on a foam pad green side up and firmly stroke each sepal from tip to middle with a dog bone tool. Turn over on to soft foam and push gently in the centre to cup. Push the rose through the calyx centre and secure to the rose base with glue. Roll a pea sized piece of paste into a cone, push onto the wire and attach to the calyx base.

6 For the leaves, roll a small grape sized piece of paste into a cigar shape. Roll thinly with a small rolling pin leaving a ridge along the centre. Cut a large rose leaf keeping the ridge down the cutter centre. Insert a hooked 28g moss green wire dipped in glue into the base of the ridge, pressing with finger and thumb. Vein by pressing on a rose leaf veiner. Soften the edges on a softening pad and vein the centre with a Dresden tool. Dry the leaves on crumpled kitchen foil.

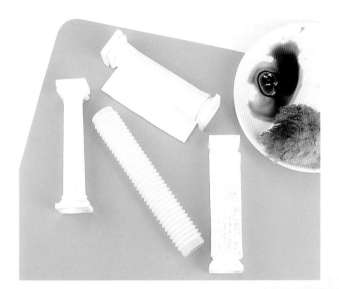

7 Measure the column length on the cake pillar. Roll out ivory frilling paste into a rectangle large enough to encircle the pillar and the same length. Roll with a ribbed rolling pin and secure around the pillar with glue. Leave to dry laid down. When dry, stipple the paste on the pillar the same as the cake surface (see step 1). Attach the pillar to the cake surface with royal icing.

8 To make the fabric effect drape, roll out ivory frilling paste to about 30 x 15cm (12 x 6in). Rub the surface with ivory pearl lustre food powder. Texture with a watered silk effect rolling pin. Gather the paste into gentle folds and attach to the front top and side with glue. Arrange the roses, leaves and crystal in the pillar and at the cake side. Attach the ribbon.

Variation

Cover a 17cm (6½in) cake card with Verdigris coloured pastillage and dry. Using a template, measure out the radial lines of the sun-dial onto the paste and draw with a black food pen. Attach black flower paste numerals around the sun-dial. Cut the fin out using template and Verdigris pastillage. Stamp out an ivy leaf design. Dry the fin, then attach to the dial with Verdigris royal icing.

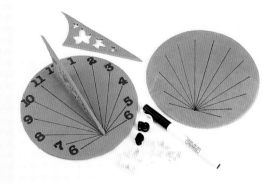

SPRING FLOWERS FOR
Mother's Day

If your mother or grandmother deserves

a really special treat for Mother's day, this

pretty spring flower cake is the one.

Bright tulips and primroses in delicate

brush embroidery decorate the pretty

panels over the cake and finely piped

flowers add a finishing touch on the

sides. Brush embroidery takes time and a

little practice, but for a beginner, the cake

will still look very effective without the

embroidery panels.

Ingredients

20cm (8in) hexagonal fruit cake, covered with melon yellow sugarpaste

225g (8oz) melon yellow sugarpaste

225g (8oz) pastillage

Royal icing

Paste food colours:
melon yellow, colonial rose, peony rose, mauve mist, forsythia, spring green, lime green, African violet, snowflake, cyclamen, melon

White vegetable fat

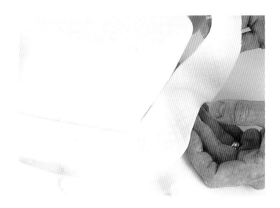

1 Roll out a band of melon sugarpaste and roll the surface with a lattice roller to texture. Trim one edge. Position the slightly elevated cake close to the textured band. Dampen the cake board and rotate the cake as you position the textured paste. Trim surplus paste from the edge of the board. Using surplus sugarpaste roll out a band measuring at least 5cm (2in) wide. Insert a grooved ring onto the side design roller then roll along the strip of paste. Trim with a cutting wheel. Lightly dust the surface of the paste with icing sugar and roll up. Dampen the base of the cake then unwind the strip, without stretching.

2 Trace the dotted outline of the template (p.108) onto thin card. Cut out with a scalpel. Colour pastillage with melon paste food colour then roll out onto a board lightly dusted with cornflour using the two pieces of mounting board as spacers. Place the template over the paste. Cut it out with the scalpel. Remove to a drying board turning occasionally, for about 24 hours. Cut out a hexagon for the centre plaque, allow to dry.

3 Trace the flower design (p.108) onto tracing paper. Trace over the back of the tracing paper. Place the tracing over the dry cut-out section then apply a light pressure as you transfer the design to the surface. A few pieces of masking tape will help keep the tracing in place while you work. If you find the lines are too dark, use a small piece of sugarpaste to gently dab the surface.

Tools and Equipment

30cm (12in) hexagonal
cake board

Side design roller

Cutting wheel

Templates

Thin card

Tracing paper

Scalpel

Two strips of mounting
board for thickness gauge

No.1 and 2 piping tubes

0 paint brush

Clear acetate

Scriber

Pink ribbon

4 To colour the design for brush embroidery, paint each section with powder food colour mixed with white/snowflake powder and water for a creamy consistency. Leave to dry before piping around each part of the design with white royal icing using a no.1 tube. Brush from the inside edge of the piped icing using a dampened paintbrush. The colour will show through the brushed icing. Add small piped dots of icing to the centre of the daisy. Apply extra shading over the brush embroidery to highlight details.

TIP

Pipe only small areas at a time when doing brush embroidery, otherwise the icing will dry and you will not be able to brush in over the coloured sections.

5 For the tulips (template p.109), fill opposite sides of a piping bag fitted with a no.2 piping tube with two shades of pink royal icing. Smear a light covering of white fat onto clear film. Pipe the tulips starting with the centre, holding the tube at a 45° angle to the surface. Pipe the two opposite petals. Pipe 50 flowers, allowing to dry thoroughly before removing from the film with a small angled palette knife.

6 For the primroses (template p.109), pipe in a similar way to the tulips but holding the tube more upright to the film. It is important to control the pressure, increasing for the outside of the petal and reducing as you move to the centre. When dry, paint a small dot of orange colour in the centre.

7 Trace the side template design (p.109) onto tracing paper. Support the cake on a tilting turntable. Secure the tracing in position with pieces of masking tape on the side of the cake. Scribe the design by making small pricks into the band of icing for the scroll design and use a sweeping action for the other design.

8 To pipe the leaves on the side of the cake, use a no.1 tube with green royal icing. Pipe over the scribed design, starting from the centre and working outwards. This will taper the tube piping.

9 To complete the larger leaves, hold the piping tube at a 90° angle to the side of the cake as you pipe. It is important that you increase the pressure as you pipe the start of the leaf, then decrease as you pull away. Attach the piped tulips and primroses with the royal icing ensuring they are raised from the surface slightly.

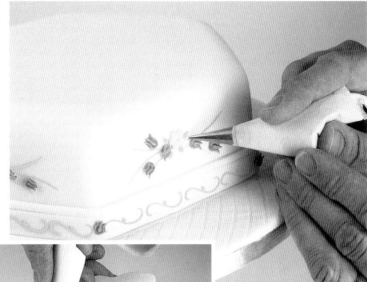

10 Scribe the message on to the plaque (p.108) then over pipe with soft green royal icing. Place each of the dry pastillage sections onto the surface of the cake to ensure that their positioning is correct before securing with royal icing. Trim the board with coloured ribbon to finish.

Variation

This cake also makes an ideal choice for a pretty birthday cake. Simply change the inscription on the hexagonal plaque to a birthday message or name. For an easier version, the cake also looks very attractive without the cut-out brush embroidery sections.

BULRUSH BABY
christening cake

This delightful baby in the bulrushes is an unusual cake for a

christening celebration, and the basic colour can easily be

changed from blue to pink. It uses a range of techniques and

takes time, but does not require advanced skills.

Ingredients

25cm (10in) teardrop shaped rich fruit cake, covered in almond paste

35cm (14in) scalloped oval blue iced board, textured with rolling pin

1.5kg (3lb 5oz) ivory sugarpaste

Sugar syrup

200g (7oz) flower paste

300g (10½ oz) frilling paste

150g (5½oz) white sugarpaste

Clear alcohol *eg* gin

Piping gel

Brown coloured semolina

Paste colours: Autumn leaf, Christmas red, gooseberry green, navy blue, liquorice, dark brown, primrose, grape violet, ivory, paprika

Powder colours: foliage green, apricot, bluebell, pink, cream

Pearl white lustre colour

Rejuvenator spirit

1 Make a template of the cake top, roll out ivory sugarpaste and cut around this template, then cover the cake. Place the pond template (p.102) in position and cut it out, cutting only the sugarpaste, not the almond paste. Lift it out, then brush the cake with sugar syrup. Cover the entire cake with ivory sugarpaste. For grass, thinly roll green flower paste and cut out various sizes of calyx. Cut each in half and divide the sepals into fronds. Soften gently with a Dresden tool. Dampen the inside edge of the pond and attach fronds around it. Place the cake on the prepared board. Mix a little blue powder colour and alcohol. Paint the base of the pond, then spread its surface liberally with piping gel.

2 For the bulrushes, cut various lengths of 20g green wire, taping each with half width tape. Roll a grape sized piece of brown flower paste into a cigar shape 3cm (1¼in) in length. Using tweezers pull out a little tail at one end, about 5mm (¼in). Insert a prepared wire into the plain end of the bulrush. Brush the bulrush with edible glue and sprinkle with brown coloured semolina. Stand to dry.

TIP

To colour semolina for adding texture, add powdered food colour and shake!

3 To make the bulrush leaves, roll out green flower paste leaving a centre ridge for the wire. Cut a leaf shape with a scalpel. Vein by pressing on to a corn leaf veiner. Insert a hooked 26g wire (dipped in glue) into the base of the ridge on the leaf, pressing as you insert. Soften the edges of the leaf on a pad and vein down the centre by pressing with a Dresden tool. Dry the leaf on a crumpled surface. For a more realistic appearance dust the leaf with moss green and cream food powders.

Tools and Equipment

Pond and leaf templates	Scalpel	Large designer wheel	Cel-stick
Calyx cutters	Cornleaf veiner	Pin	Throat former
Dresden tool	Mini quilter	Dog bone tool	Posy pick
Florists wire (20- and 26-gauge) and tape	Carnation cutters	Blossom plunger cutters	Ribbon
Tweezers	Babies head mould	Firm cotton bud stamens	
	Garrett frill cutters	Scalpel	

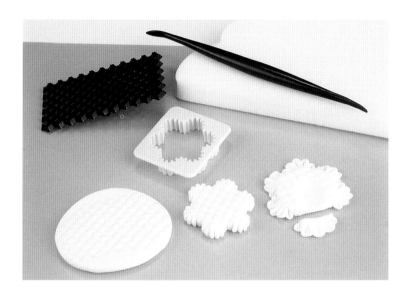

4 For the baby's pillow, roll out to 6mm (¼in) thickness white frilling paste. Emboss firmly with a mini quilter. Cut out a large carnation shape using a cutter. Press the petal edges with a Dresden tool, then cut off one petal. Hollow the centre with your finger giving baby a place to lay. Glue to one end of the leaf.

5 Mould a small amount of flesh colour frilling paste in a small head mould. Smooth the edges, neatening the base of the neck. Dry. Dust the cheeks with pale apricot, eyelids blue, lips pink. Paint the eyes with deep ivory and alcohol. Dry. Roll the white frilling paste thinly and cut 3 medium carnation shapes. Glue one to the back of the head. Frill the remaining carnation edges by rolling with a fine cel-stick and stamp out the centres with a small garrett frill cutter. Snip to single lengths and attach around the baby's head. Whilst still pliable, glue the head to the pillow. Mould a sausage of pale paprika frilling paste 4cm (1¼in) long. Taper one end and place in the leaf.

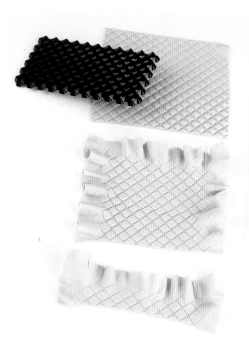

6 For the blanket, roll out a rectangle of blue frilling paste 2mm (¹⁄₁₆in) thick. Press firmly with the mini quilter. Cut around the edge of this embossing with a scalpel. Frill the edges with a small pin. Cut off a 15mm (⅝in) section from one end. Cover the baby with the large piece of blanket up to the head base. Fold in the cut edge of the smaller piece and glue in place at the top of the blanket on the baby. Dry. Paint the blanket, pillow and bonnet with pearl white lustre powder mixed with alcohol.

7 To make the large leaf, roll out autumn leaf colour flower paste. Place the leaf template (p.102) onto this and cut around with a designer wheel. Thin and soften the edges with the dog bone tool and mark the central and side veins with a Dresden tool. Curl the edges slightly with a small pin. Dry in a flower former. Dust with green powder.

TIP

Make a flower former with the inner tube of a kitchen roll cut in half lengthways.

8 To form pebbles, mould white sugarpaste with a small amount of black sugarpaste for a marble effect. Break off various sized pieces and shape into rocks and boulders. Stick these first at the front of the cake on the board, building up the cake side a little. This part of the formation holds the foundation of the bulrush. Continue around the cake base with small pebbles. Dust rock, pebble and boulder shapes with ivory and green powder food colours.

9 Roll blue, lemon or lavender flower paste thinly. Cut blossoms with large blossom cutter. Soften the edges with a dog bone tool. Cut a stamen with a round head in half, dip the head in glue and push the plain end through the flower centre. Pull down to fix firmly. Dry upside down. Dust with powder colours. Tape in threes with ⅛ width tape. Cut large calyxes from green flower paste, cut sepals and vein on foam pad. Glue to the rocks, pushing in the centre with a throat former. Fix taped blossoms in the centre.

10 Push a posy pick into the cake near the pool and add a little sugarpaste. Add bulrushes and foliage here and into the back of the rocks. Place the leaf and baby on the pond. Fix the blossoms over the cake. Attach the ribbon.

Variation

The cake can easily be changed to a birthday cake or retirement cake for a keen fisherman – use the basic shape and decoration as above, but replace the baby with a fisherman modelled from coloured almond paste, using a wooden satay stick for the rod. Place him by the pond.

BON
voyage

A farewell party to see family or friends off on a journey to

pastures new is an opportunity to show how much you'll miss

them. This bright, innovative cake, shaped as a colourful pile of

suitcases topped with sugar balloons, is an unusual

way to wish them 'Bon Voyage!'

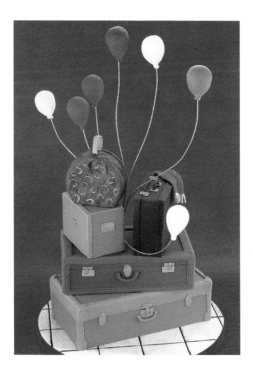

Ingredients

10-egg 20 x 30cm (8 x 12in)
rectangular madeira cake

Sugarpaste:
500g (1lb 2oz) light blue-grey
600g (1lb 5oz) golden brown
400g (14oz) dark brown
275g (9½oz) black

Buttercream

Modelling paste:
55g (2oz) black
100g (3½oz) dark brown
100g (3½oz) golden brown
100g (3½oz) pink
75g (2¾oz) white

Paste colours to paint
circular case

Edible liquid gold colour

Sugar glue

1 Cover the board with light blue-grey sugarpaste. Using a straight edged ruler, press firmly into the soft paste to form 6.5cm (2⅝in) square tiles. Use a set square to ensure the lines are perpendicular to each other. Leave to dry.

2 Mix a small amount of black sugarpaste with boiled water until it is of a piping consistency. With a paintbrush, paint the black paste into the recesses between the tiles. Remove the excess with damp kitchen paper then stipple the surface of the tiles with a clean piece of damp kitchen paper to remove the streaks. Leave to dry. Cover the reverse side of the thin cake board with dark brown sugarpaste. Dry.

3 Remove the crust from the cake base and sides then level the top to 6cm (2½in) high. Cut four rectangles and a circle as shown (right), using a set square to check that the sides are vertical. Freeze cakes. Place each cake on waxed paper and spread with buttercream before covering.

Case 1: 20 x10cm (8 x 4in)

Case 2: 18 x 9cm (7 x 3½in), height 5cm (2in)

Case 3: 8 x 6cm (3¼ x 2½in), height 4.5cm (1¾in)

Case 4: 9.5 x 7.5cm (3¾ x 3in), height 3cm (1¼in)

Case 5: 7cm (2¾in) diameter with 1cm (½in) removed from one side. Reduce height to 2.5cm (1in)

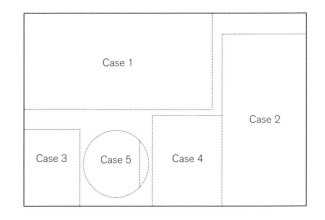

Tools and Equipment

28cm (11in) round cake board

18 x 9cm (7 x 3½in) thin cake card

Straight edge

Paintbrushes

Kitchen paper

7cm (2¾in) round cutter

Stitching wheel

Narrow spacers from stiff 15mm (⅝in) card

18-gauge white wires

Small Styrofoam balls

Dresden tool

Posy pick

Ribbon

Textured rolling pin

Scissors

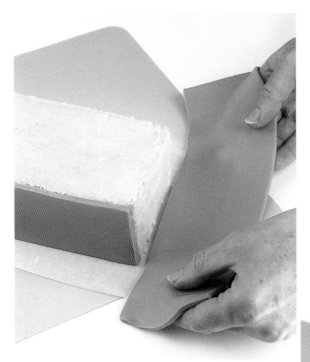

4 Roll out golden brown sugarpaste into a strip and cut one long edge straight. With the straight edge at the base, place the strip on one side of cake 1. Trim the edges flush with the uncovered sides and top of the cake. Cover the remaining sides and top. Indent the sugarpaste with straight edge at height of 4.5cm (1½in). Turn over the covered cake card so the brown sugarpaste is underneath, place cake 2 on top and cover with dark brown sugarpaste. Indent a line at a height of 4cm (1½in). Dry.

5 Roll out some golden brown sugarpaste and place cake 3 on waxed paper. Cover one long side with buttercream and place on to the sugarpaste. Cut around the case, then remove both the cake and cut paste from the paper. Cover the top, ends and remaining side in the same way. Cover case 4 with black sugarpaste. Cover the round case with golden brown sugarpaste.

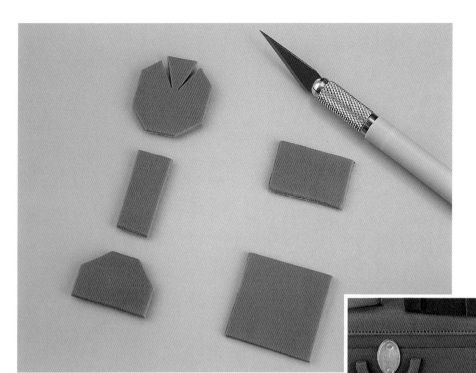

6 Roll out the remaining modelling pastes between narrow spacers. Cut into squares and strips and trim the edges and corners of the cases, abutting indented lines and covering any joins. Run a stitching wheel around the trim. Paint the round case with diluted paste colours then when dry add handles and clasps to cases. Paint clasps and locks gold.

NOTE
The balloons are not edible and should be removed before serving.

7 Cover a Styrofoam ball with sugar glue. Warm 25g (1oz) modelling paste and wrap around the ball, smoothing out joins with the heat of a finger. Roll into a ball in the palm of your hand then into a cone. Insert a wire into the cone and stroke a small amount of paste down the wire. Shape with a Dresden tool to resemble tied end of a balloon. Make as many as desired then paint the wires with liquid gold colour.

8 Place case 1 centrally on the cake board and attach cases 2, 3, 4 and the round case on top at an angle. Insert a posy pick into the centre of case 2 and insert the balloons. Bend the wires to give movement to the balloons. Thinly roll out the remaining pink modelling paste and cut to a rectangle. Cut two strips from thinly rolled white modelling paste and place one over each end of the rectangle. Texture the paste with a textured roller then cut into the white paste with scissors to create fringes. Arrange the shawl over one corner of the black case. Attach a ribbon around the board.

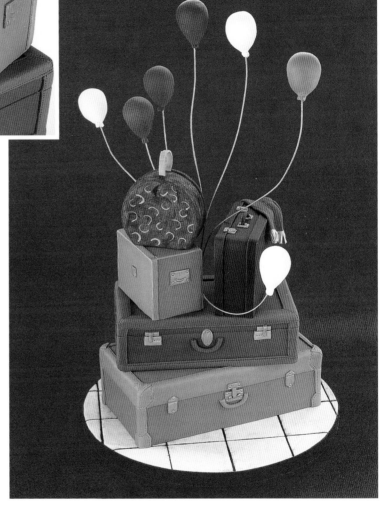

Variation

Personalise the cake by adding luggage labels or tags made from pastillage, using food colour pens to write a name or destination. For a simpler version, cut the cake into one large suitcase and cover in the same way as the small ones. Or, for a housemoving or housewarming cake, shape the cakes into packing cases instead of suitcases.

CAMELLIA *wedding* CAKE

This sophisticated, single tier wedding cake makes a superb centrepiece for a wedding table. The simplicity of the cake itself, softened by a swirl of soft tulle, is offset by the beautiful camellia flowers, modelled from flower paste. The camellias are time consuming to make, but well worth the effort, and they are a wonderful keepsake for years to come – store them in a box with grains of rice to keep them dry.

Ingredients

30cm (12in) hexagonal cake covered with Cornish cream sugarpaste

43cm (17in) hexagonal board covered with Cornish cream sugarpaste

300g (10½oz) flower paste

Edible glue

Paste food colours: foliage green, brown, cream, bluebell

Pearl white lustre

Rejuvenator spirit

Confectioner's varnish

1 Place 24 heads of fine yellow stamens along a 5mm (¼in) width of double sided tape approx 4cm (1½in) long. Lay the tip of a one third length of 30g white wire on one end. Roll up the stamens from the wire end giving a secure bundle. Make 8 per flower head.

2 Roll white flower paste very thinly leaving a centre ridge. Cut a petal shape with the smallest camellia cutter. Insert a glued, hooked 30g white wire and press on an orchid veiner. Soften the edges on a pad with a dog bone tool and vein the centre with a Dresden tool. Make 12 per flower. Dry on the crumpled foil. Repeat the process with the middle size camellia cutter using 28g wire. Make 8 per flower. Repeat for the largest camellia petal as the medium. Make 15 per flower.

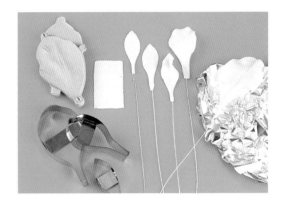

3 For the buds, mould a small grape sized piece of white flower paste into a ball and insert a length of 20g green wire taped brown. Dry. Cut out a 5cm (2in) blossom from thinly rolled white flower paste and soften the petals on a softening pad with a dog bone tool. Cup each petal by stroking tip to middle with the dog-bone. Push the dry bud through and brush the entire petals with glue. Attach each petal in a clockwise direction, enclosing the ball completely.

4 For the calyx, cut out a 2.5cm (1in) 5-petal blossom shape from thinly rolled green flower paste. Snip in between each petal towards the centre. Cup each petal with a dog bone tool. Push the bud through the calyx centre and attach with edible glue.

Tools and Equipment

Approx 200 heads fine yellow stamens

Double sided tape

30-and 28-gauge white wire and 28- and 20-gauge green wire

Camellia cutter set (incl leaf)

Orchid veiner

Dog bone tool

Dresden tool

Brown tape

2.5cm (1in), 5cm (2in) and 6cm (2½in) five-petal blossom cutters

Large calyx cutter

White lily stamens

4 posy picks

1m (39in) soft white bridal tulle

Ribbon

5 For the small, half open camellias, mould a grape sized piece of white flower paste into a ball. Tape 24 stamen heads onto a 20g green wire with brown tape half width. Pull the stamen wire through the paste ball. Dry. Repeat the petal sequence using a 6cm (2½in) as stage 3, adding an extra two sets of petals, then a calyx.

6 Make small buds from white lily stamens painted with shades of green and brown.

TIP
When modelling flowers from sugarpaste, try to obtain a fresh flower from a florist as a reference to work from.

7 For the leaves, roll a small grape size piece of green paste into a cigar shape. Thinly roll the paste leaving a ridge along the centre. Place the leaf cutter over the ridge and stamp out. Insert a glued, hooked 28g moss green wire. Soften the edges on a softening pad with a dog bone tool. Mark the central and side veins with a Dresden tool. Dry over a former, then dust with a dark green powder colour. Paint the leaves with confectioner's varnish full strength.

8 Dust all the camellia petals and buds with pearl white lustre dust on a soft brush. Dust the calyx with dark green and brown.

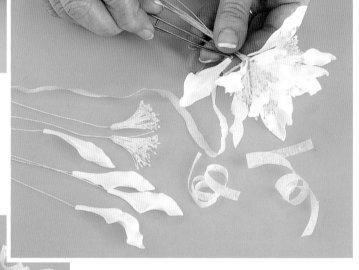

9 To assemble the camellia centre, tape 12 small petals in and around several stamen bunches, keeping closely together. Use white tape half width.

10 Add the 8 medium petals to the base of the small petals, coming slightly down the wire with the petals as you tape. Add the petals in a clockwise movement.

TIP
If you have no experience of wiring up flowers on stems, buy some inexpensive fabric flowers to practice on to get the right effect.

11 Finally, tape in the largest petals, again working a little way down the wire giving the flower a slightly domed appearance. Tape the finished camellia with brown half width tape.

12 Tape several buds down a 20g wire with half width brown tape. Add 3 buds in stages and a couple of leaves around the spray. Add an extra length of the wire if necessary. Tape into the camellia, bending the spray to accommodate. Tape extra leaves around the camellia. Insert into the cake with a posy pick. Attach the ribbon.

13 Cut a length of tulle twice the circumference of the cake, approx 30cm (12in) wide. Gather the ends and secure with 30g white wire. Divide the remainder and gather with wire to make 3 bunches. Lower over the cake with the wire gathers central to alternate sides. Push a posy pick 2.5cm (1in) above the board level central into the cake, holding down tulle. Insert a taped half open camellia bud and three leaves, concealing the wire gather.

Variation

To make a Chinese New Year celebration cake, mould white pastillage in a small cornflour-dusted bowl to make a rice bowl. Trim and dry. Paint a design with food colours and fine brush, or use food pens. To make chopsticks, push dark cream pastillage from a sugar shaper with a square disc to a length approx 15cm (6in) and cut. Carefully soften the square edges at one end. Dry. Paint a design on the flat side of each chopstick.

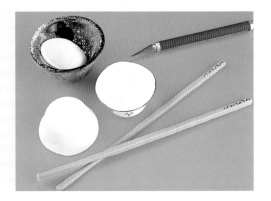

MOTORBIKE
birthday
CAKE

A motorcyclist's dream, and you can eat it, too! This realistic motorcycle is carved from madeira and covered in sections, so although it takes a little time, it's really just a matter of skilful assembly. The background benefits from an artistic hand, but could be left fairly plain if you feel you're not up to it.

Ingredients

10 egg 30 x 23cm (12 x 9in) rectangular madeira cake

Buttercream

3kg (6lb 10oz) sugarpaste:
600g (1lb 5oz) brown
900g (2lb) blue
250g (9oz) green

750g (1lb 10oz) black
150g (5½oz) yellow
300g (10½oz) grey
50g (2oz) white

235g (8½oz) modelling paste:
100g (3½oz) black

55g (2oz) grey
55g (2oz) white
25g (1oz) yellow

Paste colours for painting: range of blues, green, brown, orange, red

White and silver dust colours

Clear alcohol *eg* gin

Sugar glue

White vegetable fat

5ml (1tsp) gelatine

25g (1oz) pastillage, grey

Icing sugar

1 Roll 100g (4oz) brown sugarpaste to 5mm (¼in) thick. Dry on foam. When dry, break up to create angular rocks. To make soil, grind some smaller rocks in a pestle and mortar. Roll blue sugarpaste between 4mm (⅛in) spacers and use to cover half the board. Trim the flush with the edges of the board and cut the paste across the board. Roll the green sugarpaste into a long sausage, place between spacers, widen with a rolling pin then roll to the thickness of the spacers. Cut one edge straight and place to neatly abut the blue paste. Smooth and trim. Repeat with the brown sugarpaste. Paint sugar glue on to the brown paste around where the bike will be. Press rocks and soil into the soft paste. Leave to dry.

TIP

An airing cupboard is an ideal place to dry the paste.

2 For sky, mix blue paste colour with white dust and alcohol to make thick paint. Apply with a flat-headed paintbrush in sweeping, horizontal strokes of colour across the top of the board. Stipple over the painted area with a large dry brush to soften the effect. Add cloud traces in darker blue. For mountains, use a flat-headed paintbrush to apply darker shades of blue. Outline first then bring the colour down to sea level, creating shadow and light. For sea, apply deep blue in the foreground and lighter blue in the distance with sweeping horizontal strokes of the brush. Add a hint of surf at the base of the mountains.

Tools and Equipment

46 x 35cm (18 x 14in) rectangular cake board

4 and 5mm (⅛ and ¼in) spacers

Pestle and mortar

Narrow spacers made from card

Foam, for drying

Smoother

Painting and stippling brushes

Cutting wheel

Pan scourer

Templates

Waxed paper

Round cutters: 10, 7, 3.5cm (4, 2¾, 1⅜in)

Clear plastic sleeve

Drinking straw

Sugar shaper

Ribbon

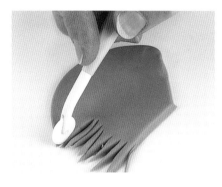

3 Add vegetation to the green strip by rolling out green sugarpaste, trimming and cutting into it with a cutting wheel to create shrubs. Attach these to either end of the green strip, so they partially cover some of the painted sea. Texture some green sugarpaste with a scourer and attach to other areas of the strip. Paint over the vegetation with diluted greens to highlight texture then paint the ground and rocks with diluted browns and black.

4 Remove the crust from the cake base and level the top to 6cm (2½in). Position the template (p.106-107), also leaving room to cut a 10cm (4in) round. Cut vertically through the cake around the template. Cut a 10cm (4in) round from the remaining cake. Cut horizontally to make two rounds for wheels, 3cm (1¼in) high. Remove the centres with 7cm (2¾in) round cutter. Freeze until firm. Mark the exhaust pipe and cut some cake from the top. Mark and shape the rear yellow panel as on the template, cutting away a small slice below and the seat area above. Shape the front yellow section and seat. Cut away the engine area and top front section. Curve the edges of the wheels with a sharp knife.

TIP
Do not worry if you slice away too much as extra pieces of sugarpaste can be added to adjust the shape when covering.

5 Place the frozen wheels on waxed paper and spread thinly with buttercream. Roll a strip of black sugarpaste between the 5mm (¼in) spacers and cut one edge straight. Wrap a strip of paste around the inside of one wheel. Cut the paste away on the top of the tyre and smooth the join closed. Roll a second strip of black paste, cut one edge straight and wrap around the outside edge of the tyre. Cut the strip to size and smooth the joins with your fingers. Smooth the tyre to give an even finish. Repeat for the second wheel. Dry.

6 Place the cake on waxed paper. Cover the front of the bike, above the yellow, with a thin layer of buttercream. Roll out some black sugarpaste between 5mm (¼in) spacers, cut one edge straight and place the straight edge along the diagonal line, on the edge of the yellow. Smooth and trim. Spread buttercream thinly over the front under section (i.e. right hand side) and cover with black sugarpaste. Trim and smooth the join. Cover and shape the following sections, spreading thinly with buttercream first: seat black, rear side of cake grey, exhaust grey, yellow panel and the rest black. Leave to dry.

7 For the windscreen, place the template (p.107) inside a plastic sleeve. Place 15ml (1tbsp) water in a small bowl, sprinkle gelatine over and add 2.5ml (½tsp) icing sugar. Dissolve over a pan of hot water. Quickly spoon the liquid over the template. Do not worry if it spreads too far as it can be trimmed. When it begins to set, trim to shape if necessary then tape the plastic sheet around a curved object, such as a narrow glass. Allow to set before removing the curved windscreen.

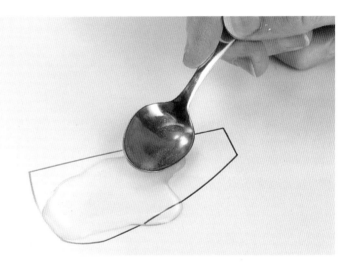

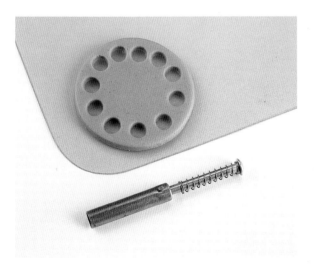

8 Roll grey pastillage thinly and cut an 8cm x 1.25cm (3¼ in x ½in) strip for the back wheel fork. Dry on foam. Colour remaining pastillage black and roll thinly. For back mudguard, cut a 4.5cm x 3cm (1¾in x 1¼in) rectangle. Dry on foam. Squeeze the remaining pastillage from a sugar shaper with a large round disc into three lengths. Keep two straight and place the third on the handlebars template (p.107). Dry on foam. Position the covered cake and wheels on the board, securing with glue. Make three 2cm (¾in) thick spokes for each wheel and attach. Cut two 3.5cm (1¼in) rounds from grey modelling paste and cut out small circles. Dry and glue to the wheels. Add a 5mm (¼in) wide strip of black modelling paste around tyres. Add balls of black paste in the centre of the wheels. Position the dried pastillage forks.

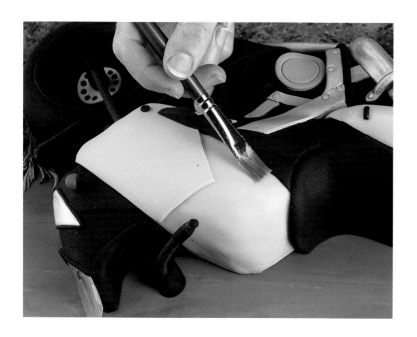

9 Add a thin layer of yellow modelling paste to the front of the front yellow section. Using a paintbrush, spread white fat over all the yellow sections. Insert the handlebar upright into cake and handlebars into the board, covering the join with additional pieces of black modelling paste. Use foam to support the handlebars whilst the glue dries. Cut the front mudguard by rolling out black modelling paste between narrow spacers, cut one edge straight and place over the front wheel. Mark the mudguard edge with a cutting wheel, remove and cut through the paste. Position slightly away from the wheel, using foam to support.

10 Colour a little white paste orange and red and model the brake and indicator light. Add a numberplate to the back mudguard and glue in place. Add detail to the end of the exhaust. Model the headlights. For the engine, add grey and black parts as desired – add as much detail as you like. Add a metallic finish to parts of the bike by painting with silver lustre dust mixed with clear alcohol. Attach the windscreen to the front of the bike. Attach a ribbon around the board.

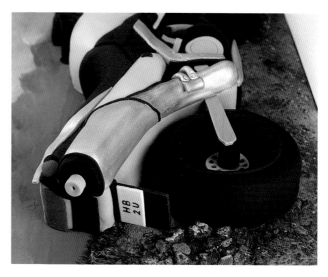

Variation

Personalise the number plate, including the recipient's name and age, such as 30 or 40, or change the model of bike and colour to suit his/her preference. If you need to feed lots of people, the background can be a whole cake as well, with the bike on top.

WINDOW BOX
birthday cake

This stunning window box, packed with remarkably realistic

flowers, would be a treat for anyone's birthday or could be

adapted for other special occasions. It's most suitable for a

fairly experienced flower modeller, although it could be

tailored to less advanced skills by changing

the flowers to simpler ones.

Ingredients

25 x 9 x 10cm (10 x 3½ x 4in) rectangular cake, covered with marine blue sugarpaste

35 x 18cm (14 x 7in) board, covered with paprika colour sugarpaste

250g (9oz) marine blue sugarpaste

200g (7oz) chocolate brown sugarpaste

300g (10½oz) flower paste

Edible glue

Yellow pollen-coloured semolina

Royal icing

Paste colours: ivory, Christmas green, dusky pink, egg yellow, navy, paprika, tangerine, gooseberry green

Powder colours: Spring green, tangerine, lemon, moss green, pink, bluebell

1 Tape six very fine lemon stamens onto a half length green wire with half width nile stemwrap. Brush the tips with glue and dip them into the yellow coloured semolina. The finished stamens should be approx 5mm (¼in) long. Cut out a tangerine flower paste daffodil trumpet shape. Frill along the longest edge with a veiner. Fold the trumpet around the end of a small rolling pin or the end of a paintbrush, glue one edge and fold over the other. Carefully tip this onto a surface to dry.

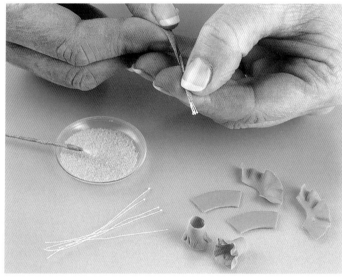

TIP

A pepperpot makes a useful fine shaker for shaking small amounts of cornflour onto a surface when flower making. Or, use a small piece of muslin tied at the top.

2 Make a Mexican hat in the yellow flower paste and use a narcissus cutter to cut one petal. Push the end of the small pin into the centre and cup against your thumb. With a veining tool roll each petal against your index finger to widen. Place upside down on foam. Vein down the centre of each petal back with a Dresden tool. Roll yellow paste and cut the second set of petals, texture, widen and vein. Brush the centre of the first petal with glue and centre the second set, lining between the first. Push into the centre with a dog bone tool. Push the wired stamens through the flower centre. Brush around the base of the stamen heads and lift the trumpet on to the flower. Holding the flower firmly push the trumpet into and over the stamen heads. Cut a narcissus flower in dark ivory flower paste and with a scalpel cut one sepal. Vein, turn over and brush the base with glue. Fold over the back base of the narcissus. Make a bulb at the flower head base with green royal icing brushed on.

Tools and Equipment

Fine yellow stamens

24-gauge nile green wire

Stemwrap

Narcissus cutter

Veiner

Dresden tool

Dog bone tool

Scalpel

Small calyx cutter

Narcissus/daffodil leaf cutter

Primrose cutter

Primrose leaf

Throat former

No.2 piping tube

Tweezers

Swag template

Scriber

Flat stipple tool

Pair marzipan spacers

Icing ruler

Seven posy picks

3 To form buds, tape two 24g nile green wire half length and half width tape. Hook the end. Roll a large pea sized piece of yellow paste into a cone shape and push in the hooked end of the wire. Dry. Roll out a narcissus shape, vein as in the centre and fold around the petals. Attach an ivory calyx as in the main flower.

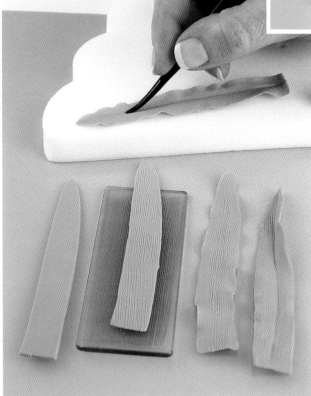

4 Cut the narcissus leaves using a cutter (or template from a real leaf), from thinly rolled pale green flower paste. Place onto a linear leaf veiner and press evenly to vein. Soften the edges with a dog bone tool on a pad, vein with a Dresden tool down the centre on soft foam. Dry on crumpled kitchen paper. When dry, dust with a bright green dusting colour and steam over a kettle.

5 For double primroses, make a Mexican hat from pale green flower paste. Cut with the small calyx cutter. Mark the centre and soften the sepals with a small rolling pin. Push a one-third length of 26g nile green hooked wire dipped in glue through the centre of the calyx. Neaten the base and place to one side. Finely roll the flower paste and cut three small primrose shapes. With scissors, cut between each petal towards the centre. With a veining tool, frill each petal over your index finger. Place on a foam pad and cup the centres. Brush the calyx with glue and attach the first petal. Repeat to attach the second and third. Push a throat former into the centre. With royal icing and a No.2 nozzle, pipe a small white dot into the flower centre.

6 Dust the narcissi and double primroses with powder colours. Steam and dry.

TIP

A crumpled piece of absorbent kitchen paper is an ideal base for drying the flower paste leaves, as it gives the leaves formation and helps drying.

7 For the primrose leaves, roll out mid green flower paste and cut out the primrose leaves. Place on a veiner and press evenly to vein. Dry over a piece of crumpled kitchen paper. When dry, dust with a dark green powdered food colour and quickly steam, holding with tweezers. Dry again on kitchen paper. Turn frequently until dry to prevent sticking.

8 Place the swag template (p.102) on front of the cake and mark gently with a scriber onto the icing. Cut small rose leaves from the blue sugarpaste, vein with a rose leaf veiner and attach to the ends of the drape. Apply the leaves overlapping towards the centre. Roll small balls of sugarpaste, cut in half and stipple for an orange peel effect. Press towards the top with a throat former. Fix at the centre of the swags with glue. Roll sugarpaste between spacers and cut 1cm (½in) widths. Dampen the base edge of the cake and apply the strip, mitreing the corners. Complete around the base and top. Emboss the covered board with an icing rule edge whilst soft.

9 Break off pieces of dark brown sugarpaste and stick onto the top of the window box. Keep the surface rough to simulate soil. Push four posy picks into the top front of the window box 4cm (1½in) from the edge. Push three more towards the back, offset from the front ones. Drop in a small piece of brown paste. Place daffodil leaves around the back three posy picks. Using tweezers insert narcissi into the posy picks, trimming the wires to vary the lengths. Insert primrose leaves around the front four posy picks, keeping the forward facing ones low and back ones higher. Cut lengths of wire to between 6cm (2½in) and 7cm (2¾in) on the double primrose and insert into the front posy picks. Fill in the spaces with foliage or flowers.

Variation

For a tropical fish enthusiast, cover the cake in pale blue/green sugarpaste and paint seaweed and fish tank detail onto the sides using food colours. Shape tropical fish from coloured sugarpaste, using flower and leaf cutters as shown.

ROMANTIC *engagement* CAKE

A classic covering of royal icing has been used here to create a distinctive cake with a contemporary style, incorporating delicate lace pieces and run-out cake top decoration, enhanced by individually wired art deco leaf shapes for a delicate, romantic effect. The cake uses several royal icing techniques and is most suitable for those with an experienced hand.

Ingredients

23cm (9in) round rich fruit cake	White vegetable fat
Apricot glaze	Paste, liquid and powder colours: pink
1kg (2lb 4oz) almond paste	125g (4½oz) pastillage
1.3kg (3lb) royal icing	25g (1oz) flower paste
Glycerine	55g (2oz) sugarpaste

1 Centre the cake card onto the flat cake base and fix a band of paper to come within 1cm (½in) of the top edge as a cutting guide. Holding a serrated knife at a 45° angle, cut the edge of the cake all the way round. Remove the paper and card.

2 Roll out a third of the almond paste using spacers. Brush the cake with apricot glaze and place upside down on the almond paste. Cut around it with a knife. Fill any indentations on the side of the cake with almond paste. Roll the remaining paste to a sausage shape about three quarters the circumference of the cake. Flatten, roll and cut to fit the side of the cake. Dust with icing sugar, roll up then unwind around the cake side, cutting to join neatly.

3 Roll the remaining almond paste into a sausage shape, then measure the width of the cut angle. Make two 45° angled cuts facing each other into the strip of paste. Secure the angled piece of paste in position then smooth over to seal joins.

> **TIP**
> Brush apricot glaze thinly and evenly, as if you use too much it may seep through the joints of almond paste and cause the royal icing to discolour.

> **TIP**
> To remove any rough edges from royal icing when dry, gently rub with fine sandpaper.

4 Add 1tsp (5ml) glycerine to each 450g (1lb) royal icing for coating. Apply the first coat of royal icing to the top of the cake, levelling off with a ruler, keeping the edges clean. Repeat on the side of the cake. Leave to dry then apply the coating to the angled edge, holding the side scraper at a 45° angle whilst rotating the turntable. Repeat to give three coats. Apply three coats of icing to the board (see p.16).

Tools and Equipment

20cm (8in) cake card

Serrated knife

8mm (⅜in) spacers

Palette knife

Side scraper

Icing ruler

33cm (13 in) cake board

No.1 and 2 piping tubes

Run-out film

Angle poise lamp with 60 watt reflector bulb

13cm (5in) circle of thin card

9cm (3½in) round cutter

Drinking straw

Small paintbrush

Scalpel

White 30 gauge wires

Art deco leaf and ribbon tail cutter

White florist tape

1.25m (1½yards) ribbon

5 Trace the lace design (p.110) onto a strip of white paper. Place under run-out film, smeared with a light covering of white vegetable fat to allow the design to be moved along. Pipe the outline with white, then pink, royal icing using a no.1 piping tube. Position an angle poise lamp 25cm (10in) from the surface and leave to dry.

6 Trace the top decoration (p.109), embracing couple and collar (p.110). Place under run-out film and outline in royal icing with a no.1 piping tube. Thin the icing with water until it holds it's shape for about 6 seconds. Cover and leave for 30 minutes. Colour part of the icing with liquid colour. Using a no.1 piping tube, flood the heart shapes on the collar, and the female shape on the embracing couple. Place under the lamp to skin over, about 30 minutes, then flood the remaining section. Leave to dry completely for about 24 hours. Slide a thin palette knife under the run-out pieces. Flood the other side of the figures in the same way.

7 Knead the pastillage and roll to 2mm (⅛in) thickness. Cut circles using the 13cm (5in) circle of card and 9cm (3½in) cutter. Cut out the small hole in the smaller circle with a drinking straw. Place on a drying board, turning regularly whilst drying to prevent buckling. Cut a strip of pastillage 2cm (¾in) wide and long enough to go inside the 9cm (3½in) cutter. Dust the cutter with cornflour then place the strip of paste inside, making a neat butt joint.

8 Cut white 30 gauge wire to 16, 14, 12, 10, 8 and 6cm (6¼, 5½, 4½, 4, 3¼ and 2½in) lengths. Roll out flower paste and cut out with a small art deco leaf cutter. Insert the end of the wire into the cut shapes. When dry, shape to a curve with a 90° angle at the base. Dust with powder colour then tape in decreasing sizes into the curved spray. Make two in opposite directions, then join together.

9 Divide the circumference of the cake using a band of paper into six sections, then fold up into one section. Trace the template (p.109) for the graduated line work onto one section then cut out with scissors. Secure the template to the side of the cake with a small piece of masking tape. Pipe around the template using a no.1 piping tube and soft white royal icing. Remove the template, then pipe a line inside with a no.1 piping tube. Over pipe the no.2 with the no.1.

10 Mix equal parts of flower paste and sugarpaste for the side decoration. Colour two thirds pink. Roll out thinly then use an art deco petal cutter to cut six pieces, placing each under a plastic container until ready to use, to prevent drying out. Make one cut at the base, then lift the edges in opposite directions. Cut the art deco leaf shapes and ribbon tail pieces in white and pink paste.

11 Secure to the art deco petal section with sugar glue then secure to the side of the cake between the paper template. Pipe a small bulb of icing at the top edge of the cake then position each piece of lace horizontally to the edge.

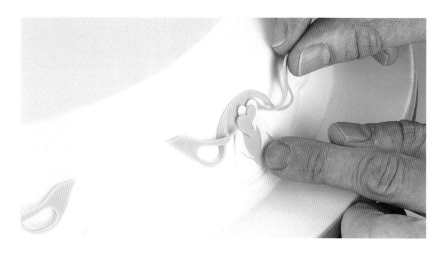

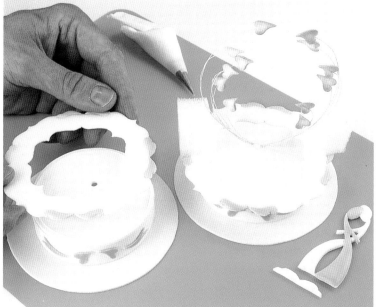

Variation

Instead of the romantic silhouette of the embracing couple, run-out numerals could be used for an 18th birthday celebration, or a 25 for a silver wedding anniversary, adapting the colours as necessary.

12 For the top decoration, smooth the edges of the pastillage. Secure a band of pastillage in the centre of the larger circle with soft white royal icing. Add a second circle, placing the small hole parallel with the join. Cut leaf shapes and opposite ribbon tail pieces and apply to the side, repeating four times around the band of paste. Pipe a line of royal icing around the top edge to secure the collar. Insert the wired leaf spray into the hole, securing it with sugar gunge (softened pastillage with sugar glue). Attach the embracing couple with royal icing when the wired spray is set. Secure the small piece of run-out at the base of the couple to strengthen and hide the joints. Attach the ribbon.

GOLDEN WEDDING
anniversary

A Golden Wedding celebration is often one of the biggest celebrations in any family, so here's a very beautiful design to fit the happy occasion. In a soft base colour, the oval cake is finished with a soft swirl of lacy sugarpaste and topped with a classical rose bud and hypericum arrangement. The unusual icing extension around the sides is achieved with scroll link twist cutters, and there's a touch of gold in tiny golden droplets.

Ingredients

30cm (12in) oval cake, covered with almond paste

2kg (4lb 8oz) sugarpaste

Royal icing

100g (3½oz) pastillage

140g (5oz) flower paste

Paste food colours: pale cream, pale green

Powder colours: pale green, tangerine, burnt orange, chestnut brown, gold

Tylose or c.m.c. powder

Sugar glue

Confectioner's glaze

White vegetable fat

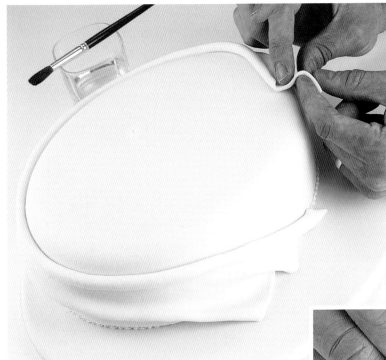

1 Cover the cake and board with cream sugarpaste (see pp.16-17), placing the cake off-centre on the cake board. Leave to dry. Add 5ml (1tsp) Tylose powder to 450g (1lb) cream sugar paste, to give more stretch for the drape. Roll out the paste and taper the cut of the drape so that it wraps around the front and back, curving onto the surface of the cake. First cut the paste roughly to shape, then place it onto the cake surface and make minor adjustments to the size with scissors. Make the folds then secure in position with sugar glue.

2 Colour royal icing a pale cream, fill a piping bag fitted with a no.1 piping tube to pipe filigree work over the drape, which will add texture.

Tools and Equipment

40cm (16in) cake board

No.1 piping tube

Scroll link twist cutter

Dresden tool

Scalpel

Card templates

Medium rose petal cutter

Small blossom cutter

Light green 24-, 26- and 30-gauge wires

Tapered stick

Ball tool

Gold wire

5cm (2in) Styrofoam ball

Green tape

Angled tweezers

1.5 m (1⅝yards) gold ribbon

3 Mix approximately 50g (1¾oz) sugarpaste with an equal amount of flower paste then colour a pale cream. Roll out thinly on a non-stick board, allowing to rest for a couple of minutes before turning the paste over and cutting out (this gives a better cut and helps to keep it in shape). Cut 12 pieces with a scroll link twist cutter, using the Dresden tool to ease out the paste. Ensure all of the cut pieces are facing the same way on the board prior to picking each one up and twisting in the centre section. Return to the rolling board.

4 Brush sugar glue onto the back of each twisted scroll. Starting at the front of the cake, secure each piece as you gradually progress around the side of the cake. Leave to dry for about two hours. Pipe the drop extension lines from one scroll to the next. Pipe small droplet shapes onto non-stick paper, leave to dry then brush with gold colour. Attach with soft royal icing.

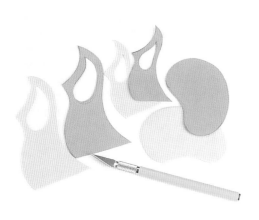

5 Colour the pastillage a pale cream, then roll out to approximately 15mm (⅝in) thickness and place the card templates (p.110) over. Using a scalpel, carefully cut out the sections allowing them to dry for at least 24 hours, turning them occasionally during drying.

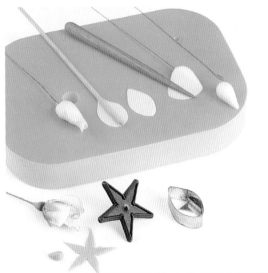

6 For the roses, cut 24g green wires in half and hook at one end. Shape cream flower paste to a cone, inserting a hooked wire into the base. Place the cone of flower paste on a rolling board. Using a tapered stick, roll out the right hand edge of the rose cone, large enough to form one petal. Curl round the cone, securing with glue. Cut five more petals, rolling from the centre of each petal towards the outside edge with a tapered stick. Secure two, then three petals around the cone fairly tightly. Cut a calyx making a small cut on each section. Thin, then apply to the bud. Make a small cone of paste for the sepal securing to the rose base with glue. Colour dust and steam.

TIP

Steaming lightly after dusting with powder colour will help to fix the colours.

7 For the hypericum, cut each piece of 26g green wire into four. Shape pale cream flower paste into small grape sized pieces. Insert a wire from the base of each, pushing out of the top by about 1mm (½₂in). Colour dust with pale green, tangerine and burnt orange. Colour the tips with chestnut brown. Cut the blossom pieces from pale green, cutting a small 'v' shape between the petals. Place on foam and elongate each petal using a ball tool. Cup the petals, turn over and secure onto the berries. Dip into light confectioner's glaze and dry upside down. Make leaves using same technique as for ivy leaves (*below*), but cut with a scalpel. Colour dust then steam lightly.

TIP

To roll flower paste as thinly as possible, it helps to smear the work surface with a thin film of white vegetable fat.

8 For the ivy, cut each 30g green wire into four pieces. Colour flower paste pale green, then insert a wire half way into the paste. Transfer to a rolling board. Flatten the sausage of paste with a small palette knife, then roll on each side of the wire. Cut ivy leaf shapes, thin the edges then leave to dry on a piece of crumpled cling film. Mix green powder colour with water, brush over one side of the leaf and while still wet scratch away the leaf veins. Brush pale green powder on the reverse of the leaf then apply a light confectioner's glaze.

9 Use gold wire to form the numerals 50, using a pair of pliers to pinch the two ends together.

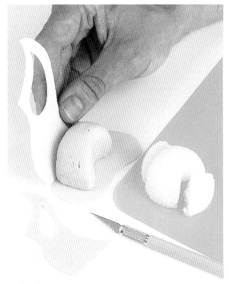

10 Take a pea sized piece of pastillage and soften with water to make a sugar gunge. Take the Styrofoam ball, cut in half and take a small slice from the rear and a 'v' shaped wedge from the front. Cover with a mixture of half flower paste and half sugarpaste. Secure each of the dry sections of pastillage onto the base.

11 Tape the stem of each flower and leaf with one third width pale green tape. Cut the flowers to length, then insert into the covered Styrofoam with angled tweezers. Insert the golden numerals, then pipe matching filigree icing onto the Styrofoam sphere. Attach the ribbon.

Variation

For a silver wedding celebration, replace the gold wire with a silver wire '25'. For a different effect, twist the wire around a bamboo skewer when shaping the numbers. Replace the gold droplets with silver instead, and finish the cake with a silver ribbon.

templates

This selection of templates covers all the designs used in the cakes in this book. To use them, simply trace onto tracing paper then transfer to card, or photocopy instead.

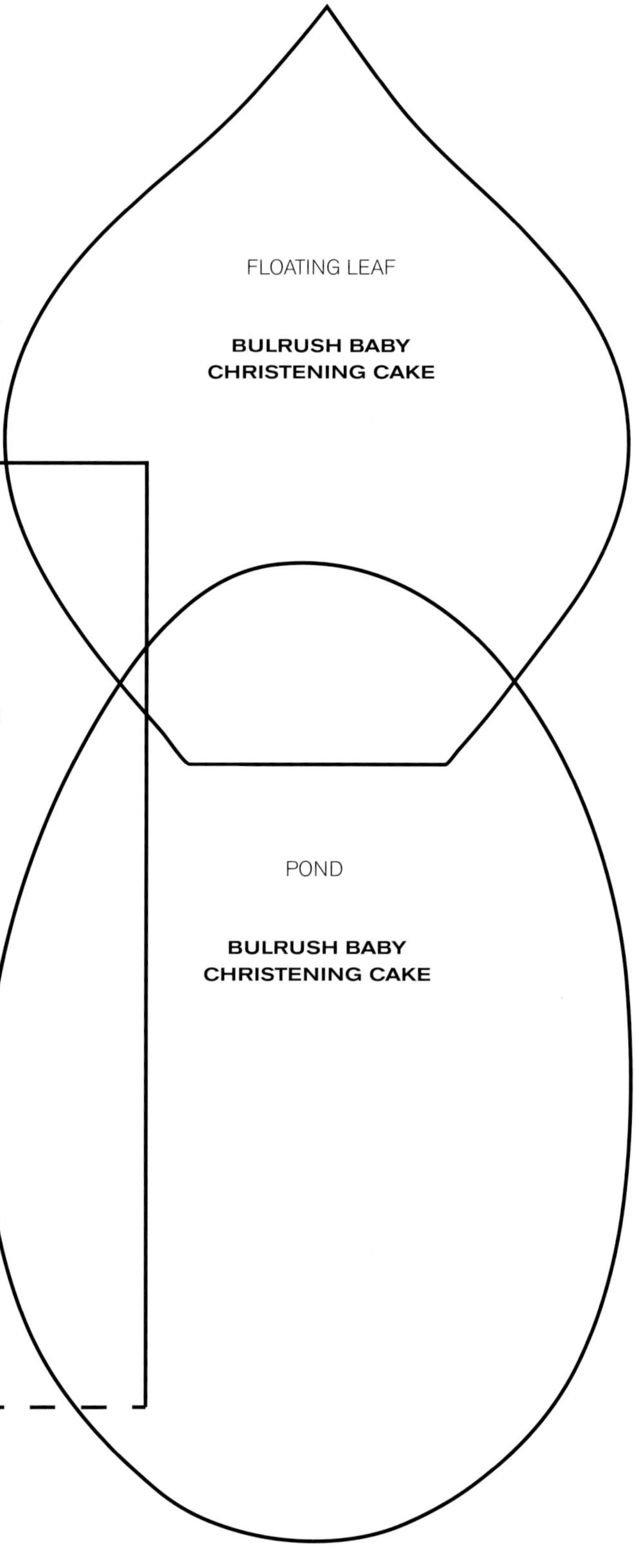

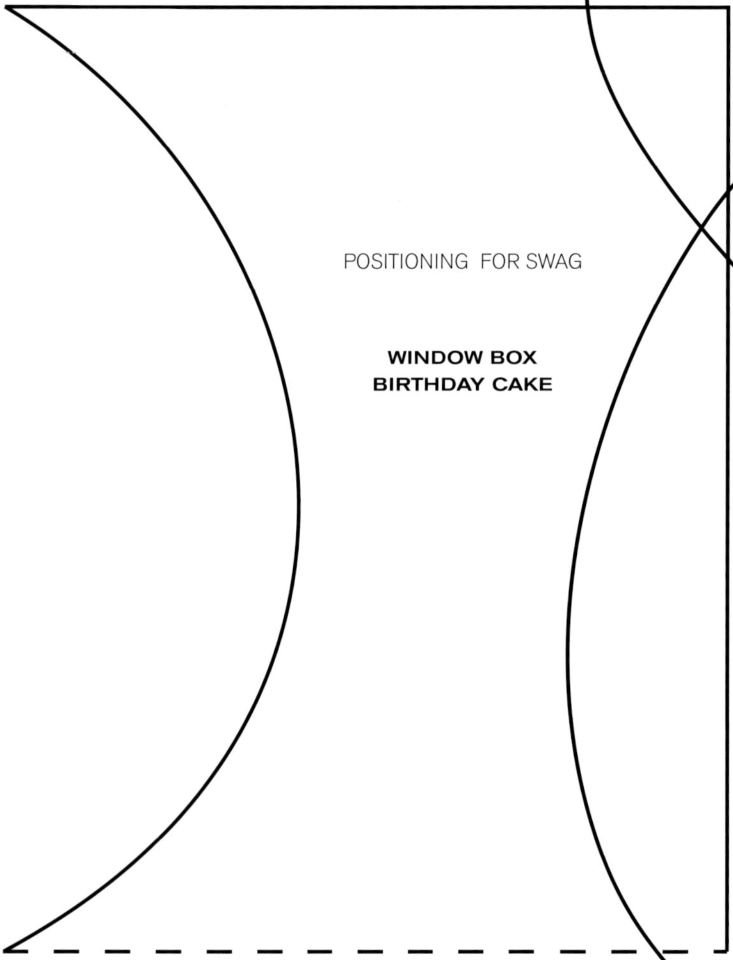

FLOATING LEAF

BULRUSH BABY CHRISTENING CAKE

POSITIONING FOR SWAG

WINDOW BOX BIRTHDAY CAKE

POND

BULRUSH BABY CHRISTENING CAKE

**SKATEBOARDING
SOCCER PLAYER**

1

2

3

4

1

2

4

3

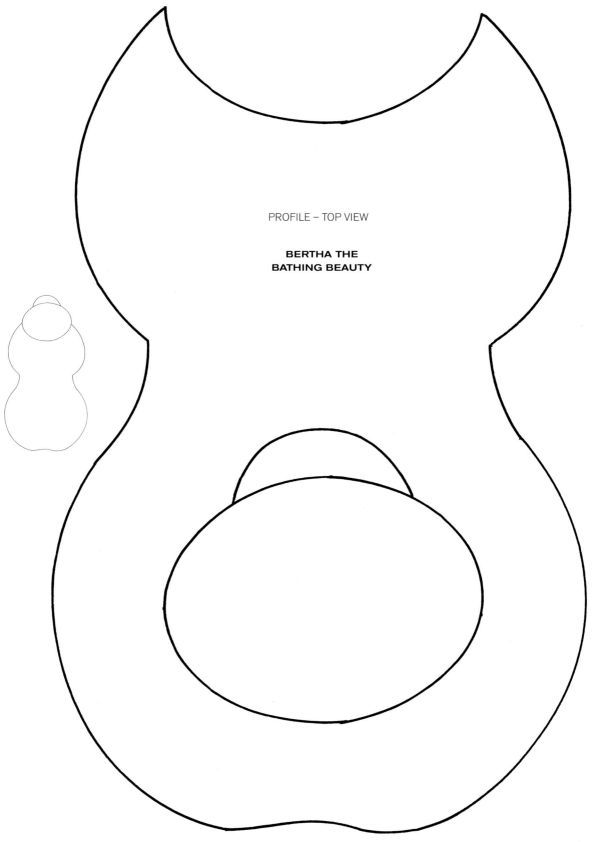

PROFILE – TOP VIEW

**BERTHA THE
BATHING BEAUTY**

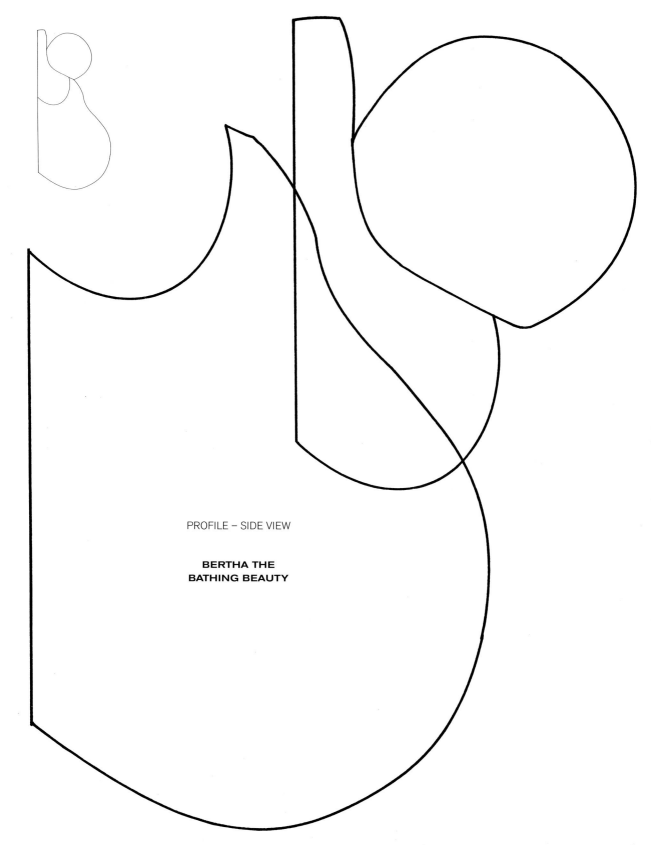

PROFILE – SIDE VIEW

**BERTHA THE
BATHING BEAUTY**

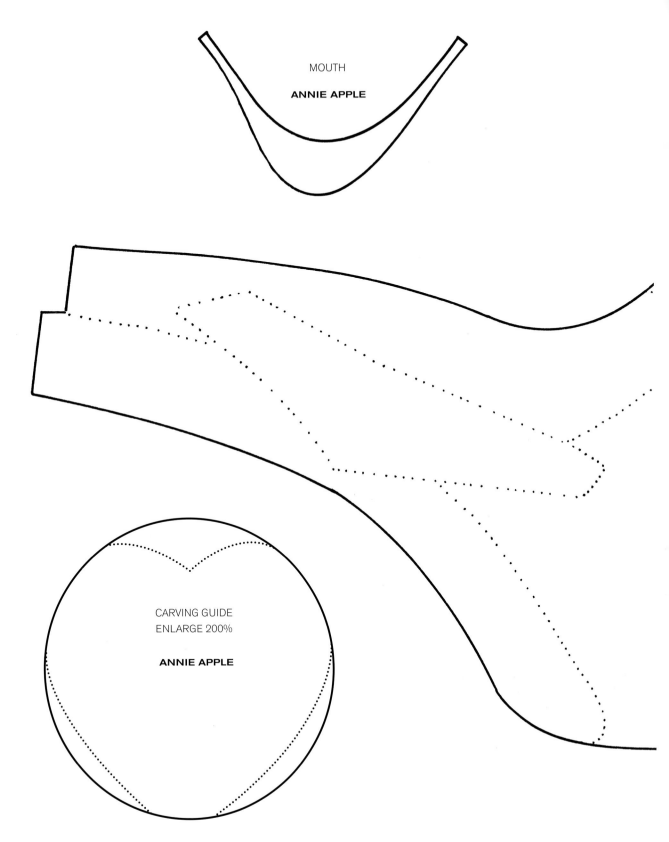

MOUTH

ANNIE APPLE

CARVING GUIDE
ENLARGE 200%

ANNIE APPLE

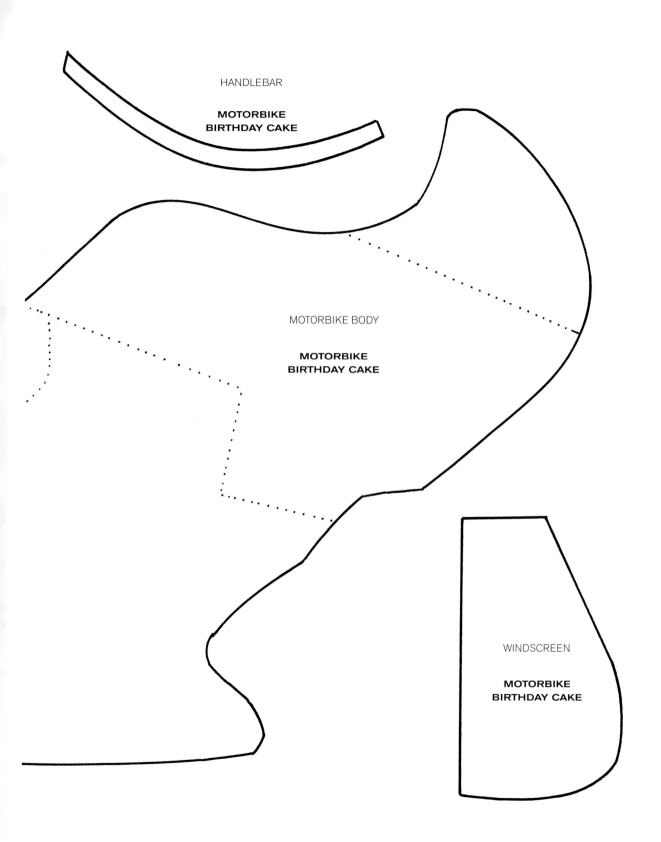

HANDLEBAR

**MOTORBIKE
BIRTHDAY CAKE**

MOTORBIKE BODY

**MOTORBIKE
BIRTHDAY CAKE**

WINDSCREEN

**MOTORBIKE
BIRTHDAY CAKE**

DIVISIONAL
GUIDE

**RETIREMENT
CAKE**

ARCH

DOOR

**RETIREMENT
CAKE**

GATE

**RETIREMENT
CAKE**

On Your

Retirement

INSCRIPTION

**RETIREMENT
CAKE**

To Mum

With

Love

BRUSH EMBROIDERY DESIGN

**SPRING FLOWERS
FOR MOTHER'S DAY**

INSCRIPTION

**SPRING FLOWERS FOR
MOTHER'S DAY**

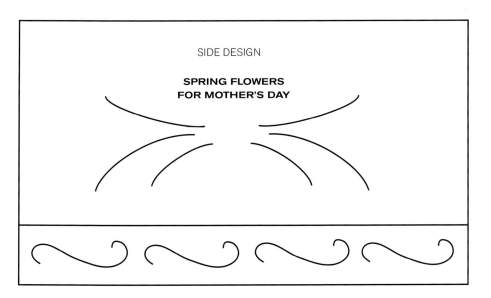

SIDE DESIGN

**SPRING FLOWERS
FOR MOTHER'S DAY**

**SPRING FLOWERS
FOR MOTHER'S DAY**

TULIP   PRIMROSE

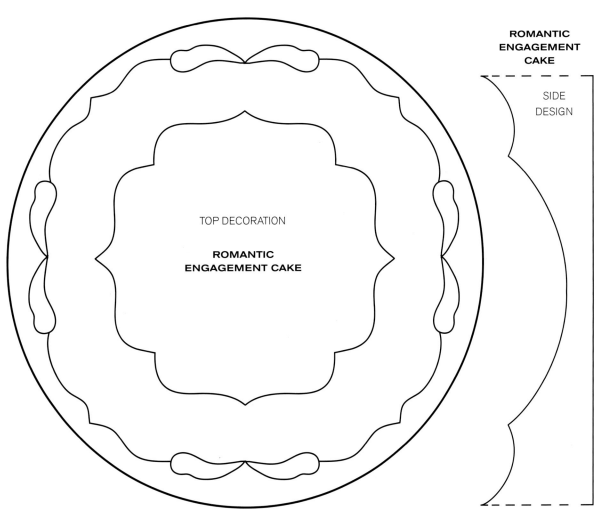

TOP DECORATION

**ROMANTIC
ENGAGEMENT CAKE**

**ROMANTIC
ENGAGEMENT
CAKE**

SIDE
DESIGN

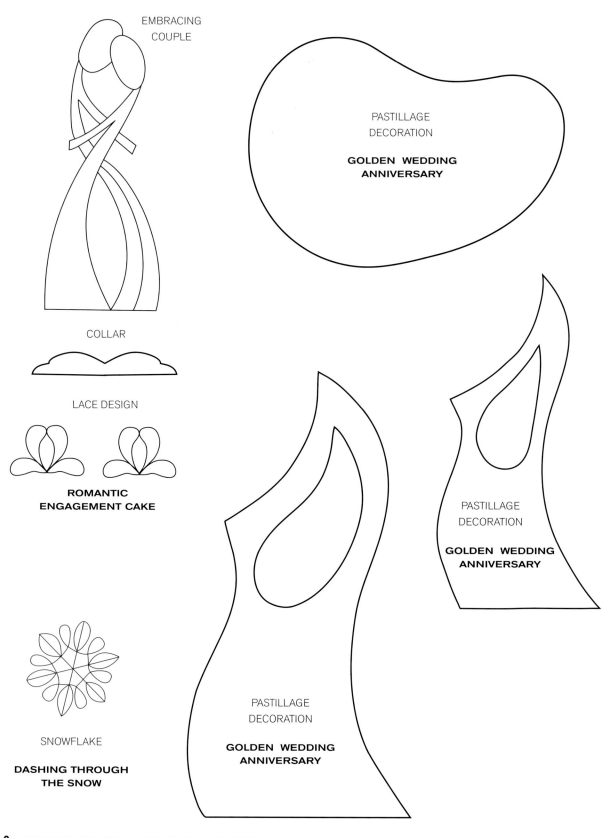

EMBRACING COUPLE

PASTILLAGE DECORATION

GOLDEN WEDDING ANNIVERSARY

COLLAR

LACE DESIGN

ROMANTIC ENGAGEMENT CAKE

PASTILLAGE DECORATION

GOLDEN WEDDING ANNIVERSARY

PASTILLAGE DECORATION

GOLDEN WEDDING ANNIVERSARY

SNOWFLAKE

DASHING THROUGH THE SNOW

suppliers

Cel-Stick non-stick pins
Celcrafts, Springfield House, Gate Helmsley, York YO4 1NF

Numeral cutters, mini quilter
Patchwork Cutters, 3 Raines Close, Greasby, Wirral, Merseyside CH49 2QB

Cake decorating equipment
A Piece of Cake, 18-20 Upper High Street, Thame, Oxon OX9 3EX

Flower, leaf and designer cutters, tools, flower and pastillage paste mixes, ribbons
Sugarworks FineArt Products, 1 & 2 Dudley Street, Kidderminster, Worcs DY10 2JJ

Corn leaf veiner, throat former
JEM Cutters C.C, PO Box 115, Kloof 3640, South Africa

Leaf veiners
Culpitt Ltd, Jubilee Ind Est, Ashington, Northumberland NE63 8UQ

Specialist cutters, scroll link twist, art deco leaf and ribbon tail, side design roller and art deco petal cutter
Stephen Benison, 28 Rodwell Park, Trowbridge, Wiltshire BA14 7LY

Vari-pin
Orchard Products, 51 Hallyburton Rd, Hove, East Sussex BN3 7GP

Moulds, confectioner's varnish, piping gel, tools
Guy Paul & Co Ltd, Unit B4 Foundry Way, Little End Rd, Eaton Socon, Cambs PE19 3TR

Stamens and wires
The Old Bakery, Kingston St. Mary, Taunton, Somerset TA2 8HW (plus most types of cake decoration equipment)

Food colours and pens, rejuvenator spirit
Sugarflair Colours Ltd, Brunel Road, Manor Trading Est, Benfleet, Essex EX7 4PS

Sugarpaste and almond paste
Renshaw Scott Ltd, Crown Street, Liverpool L8 2RF

Primrose leaf veiner
Great Impressions, Green Lea, 14 Studley Drive, Swarland, Morpeth, Northumberland NE65 9JT

Tools, designer wheel, bell mould, piping tubes
PME Sugarcraft, Brember Road, South Harrow, Middlesex HA2 8UN

Sugar shaper
B & D Manufacturing, Aldershot, Hants

---

acknowledgments

Stephen Benison would like to thank British Bakels Ltd, Granville Way, Off Launton Road, Bicester, Oxon OX6 0JT, for supplying the sugarpaste used for all his projects. www.sugar-artistry.co.uk

Lindy Smith would like to thank Christine Last for introducing her to the work of Beryl Cook which inspired Bertha the bathing beauty and her husband, Graham, for all his help with the design research. www.lindyscakes.co.uk

Linda Wilson-Barker would like to thank her husband Tony and son Phil for all the help and encouragement with the project. Also thanks to Lynn for covering the trade at her business whilst she was involved with the work.

She dedicates her work in this book to her late mother Jean Hughes-Hubbold with love.
Thanks go to all the suppliers and manufacturers for use of their tools and equipment, and especially Christine and Don for their patience during the photo shoots!
www.sugarworksonline.com

index

A DAVID & CHARLES BOOK

First published in the UK in 2003

Copyright © Steve Benison,
Lindy Smith, Linda Wilson-Barker
2003

Photography by Don Last

Distributed in North America
by F&W Publications, Inc.
4700 E. Galbraith Rd.
Cincinnati, OH 45236
1-800-289-0963

Steve Benison, Lindy Smith,
Linda Wilson-Barker have asserted
their rights to be identified as
authors of this work in accordance
with the Copyright, Designs &
Patents Act, 1988.

All rights reserved. No part of this
publication may be reproduced,
stored in a retrieval system, or
transmitted, in any form or by any
means, electronic or mechanical, by
photocopying, recording or otherwise,
without prior permission in writing
from the publisher.

A catalogue record for this book is
available from the British Library.

ISBN 0 7153 1471 8 (hardback)
ISBN 0 7153 1644 3 (paperback)

Printed in Hong Kong by Dai Nippon
for David & Charles
Brunel House Newton Abbot Devon